HIGH IMPACT HOSPITALITY

Upgrade Your Purpose, Performance, and Profits

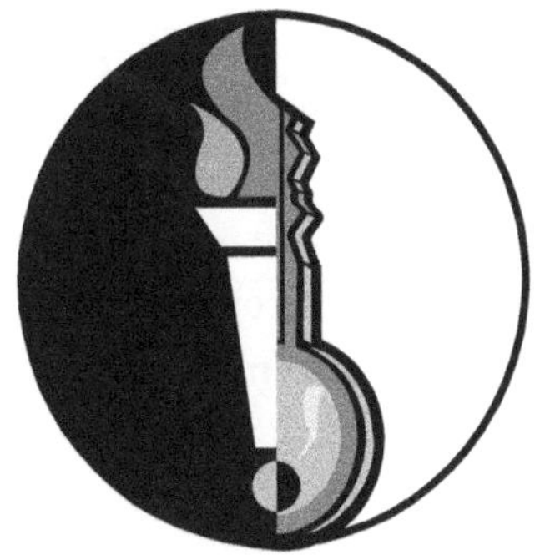

CHASE L. LEBLANC
Founder & CEO, LEADAGERS LLC

Thundersnow Publishing
Lakewood, Colorado

First printing 2010

ISBN 978-0-9843818-2-1

LCCN 2010923748

ATTENTION CORPORATIONS, UNIVERSITIES, COLLEGES, AND PROFESSIONAL ORGANIZATIONS: Quantity discounts are available on bulk purchases of this book for educational, gift purposes, or as premiums for increasing magazine subscriptions or renewals. Special books or book excerpts can also be created to fit specific needs. For information, please contact www.Leadagers.com.

To everyone I have encountered along the way,
I have learned something from each of you.
Some of you taught me more about myself.
Some of you taught me more about yourself.

To Alexa, Kit, and C.J.
Always be sunshine-makers, not jellybean-takers!

To Kristi—44 infinity

Thanks to Sue Collier and her team at S.P.R. for helping to make this book happen, including Kate Deubert, as well as Dan Forrest-Bank, who designed this eye-catching book cover.

Thanks to all my manuscript elves: Kristi LeBlanc, Gwen Mills, Dr. Douglas Mills, Lee Jette, John Ryan, and Chuck Holcomb.

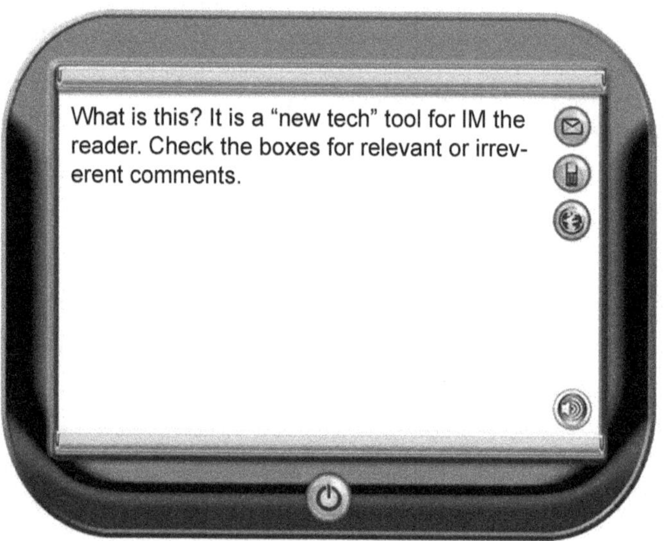
What is this? It is a “new tech” tool for IM the reader. Check the boxes for relevant or irreverent comments.

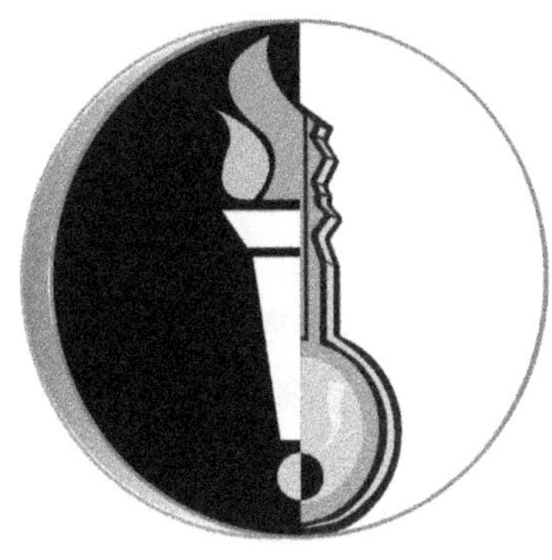

TABLE OF CONTENTS

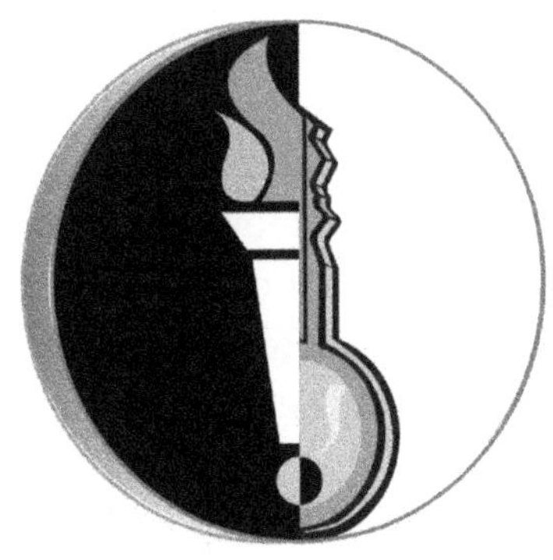

INTRODUCTION

I once had a beast of a dog, a 125-pound, all-black German shepherd named Dakota. He was foreboding in the looks department but in reality he was just a big marshmallow. Dakota would frequently do the oddest thing; whenever we were standing close together, he would lean on me. His weight was enough to shift my center of gravity and at times I would have to scramble to regain my footing.

At one of his annual veterinary check-ups, I asked the vet whether this posture was common for big dogs looking to take a load off or if this dog just liked being close to me. The vet told me that it is the nature of dogs to slide up against each other and test the weight of the newcomer. I guess my dog was on instinct autopilot, subtly trying to test the competition in case there was going to be a tussle.

I don't know if the vet was dealing in facts but I like to use this analogy when speaking about management and leadership. There is always something sliding up next to you trying to test your mettle. You are being constantly tested and assessed by the staff, customers, budget, boss, or competition—even your peers.

This book is about giving you a healthy dose of heft. After almost thirty years in the industry I'm hoping to share the solid footing that comes from hard-won wisdom.

Over time, with hands-on experience, I have come to understand that I prefer to work with authentic, caring, trustworthy, and competent people. People who do not possess these traits generally seem to fail at a higher rate. As such, I devoted much of my career to developing myself and my managers into people who were successful (by my assessment and by those who signed our paychecks) even though most of the time, we heard different music in our heads. I call us *leadagers* (leed/i/jers), and we are a tribe, a group united by our shared values.

Let's be clear; not everyone who has worked for me has liked me and certainly not everything I touched turned to gold. However, from the beginning, I was driven to produce more *leadagers* and leaders, not just more managers or hourly workers. It was somewhere at about the eleven-year mark that I began to realize I excelled in the development of *leadagers.*

As an owner/operator running a college town hot spot, I got started developing people when I was twenty-one years old. I was learning from my management mistakes before most people get a chance to make 'em. (Check out Malcolm Gladwell's book, *Outliers,* and look up the 10,000-hour rule of thumb. He basically states that ten years of practice is just about how long it takes to become really good at something.)

It's not like I ignored any of the million little details that go into running a successful hospitality operation; you have to *know* the right thing to do to *teach* the right thing to do. It's just that developing managers into strong leaders is what I poured my heart into.

I come forward now with this humble effort, targeting the following audiences: (1) assistant managers looking for more traction on their way up the mountain, (2) any level of manager in the service sector (general or multi-unit included) who is trying to improve their plate-spinning abilities, (3) hourly tribemates with ambition, and (4) anyone wishing for a peek into the mind of a "new-style" manager.

Let me be clear: There is no one right way to be successful in this industry or any other, for that matter. This book is an answer to many questions but it is not the answer to all problems.

With that in mind, may my mistakes help you to avoid some pitfalls, my knowledge be a force for good, and my travails tickle your fancy.

(Damn, I loved that dog!)

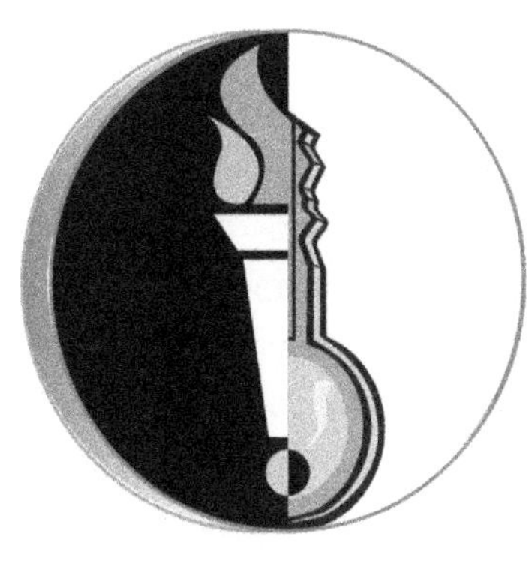

Chapter 1

A Fresh-Baked Perspective

If you ask a hundred people to define leadership, most will start by giving an example of a historical figure: "Hmmm, you know, like hmmm...Martin Luther King, Gandhi, hmmm...Abraham Lincoln... or Winston Churchill." They will list superstars who have had superb achievements on the world stage and usually in the fields of politics, religion, or the military. Quotations from the "great leaders" become rally-cry standards, recognizable within two or three beats, as in, "I have a dream...." "Ask not...." "We shall fight...." "Four score and seven...."

So what is leadership? Is it timing, luck, pluck, a function of power, shared values in action, charisma, vision, cunning, influence, cleverness, pure heart/dark heart, clarity of thinking, communication skills, driven by situational transactions or genetically coded behavior? Maybe it's an artful favor exchange program or just plain, new-fashioned "street cred." If you were to study great leaders throughout history you'd find that irrespective of how they each powered their accomplishments, it is clear there isn't a singular approach or even a straightforward way to play the cards from the above deck.

For the sake of continuity in this book, let's cut through the many years of study and dissection on this subject matter and agree that...

If you are a leader, your actions or ideas are out in front; and for the purpose of our discussion, they must also add value to the organization.

Leaders reveal themselves by doing what they *should do,* pushing beyond the artificial limitation of "what can I *possibly do?*"

Leadership can be top-down, bottom-up, or sideways, and no matter the scope or style, great leadership exists on small, medium, and large scales.

Leadership is a role, not a job title. It is not universally listed on the human resource department's "people-power" vacancies. Rarely, if ever, is one hired as an assistant leader or general leader.

Further, as a leader on our list, your first "job" is to manage *yourself* toward "betterment." (Because a crack/crank pipe rolling around under the front seat of your car, not paying your taxes, stealing company funds, DUI arrests, or pornography addictions will surely serve as distractions from your "message." Perhaps more significantly, it will evermore hurt your credibility, thereby diminishing buy-in and ensuring that you will travel the bumpy road of self-inflicted trauma.)

Between management and leadership, leadership always gets the sugar. "Great leaders" are publicized and romanticized as their reputations grow oversized.

So what of the lonesome manager who with minimal notoriety and in relative obscurity toils away far from the world stage? Imagine the chuckles that would accompany the following introduction: "Ladies and gentlemen, allow me to present the manager of the free world." It just seems to flow better when you say "leader of the free world." The ironic thing is that if you were the president of the United States, you would actually have to be a superb *manager* to be successful.

Being a manager *is* a job title (e.g., department manager, deli manager, line manager, shift manager, general manager, and so on). Most managers' achievements are unusually modest when they are measured against winning wars, building empires, or curing diseases. And few, if any, have given world-class speeches. (Can you imagine a speech from a classic movie starting off like this? "We shall fight the cost of production 'til our final breath. I have a dream of same store sales up 20 percent over last year. Ask not what your manager can do for you; ask what you can do for your manager.")

Whether you view the job of manager as being indispensable or reprehensible, you would likely agree that most people working under the job title of "manager" don't alter the arc of history during the course of a career. However, based on the sheer number of individuals working as a manager, it is obvious that collectively they most assuredly move the dial of progress.

THE ORIGIN OF "*LEADAGER*"

Can you be a leader without being a manager? The answer is yes (that's called a figurehead). Can you be a manager without being a leader? The answer is yes, if your job does not involve managing people. Can you be a *great* manager without being at least a decent leader? If your job involves managing people in any way, shape, or form, the answer is no.

It takes a certain kind of manager to apply him- or herself to becoming a great leader. You could be a "natural" and all the aforementioned is part of your flow. Perhaps you have decided to stretch and grow your professional breadth and depth or maybe you have heard you are about to get the boot if you don't improve your leadership skills.

Most managers do not envision themselves to be world-class leaders although that is entirely possible. If you have a job and a title, you are usually busy going about your duties. If you are a good manager (with a touch—or more—of leadership ability) you can usually make a nice living for yourself.

Let me take a moment to explain why leadership gets all the sugar. In the sporting world, you have certainly heard the glum billionaire owner offer up the excuse of a "lack of leadership in the locker room" after highly paid talent performed poorly on the field of play. What's up with that? World-class talent, a quad-million dollar paycheck, and a rich tradition—and they can't do it by themselves?

Bad Team + Great Leader = Better Team
Bad School + Great Leader = Better School
Bad Store + Great Leader = Better Store

Great leadership can quicken the transformation from losers to winners, no matter how you keep score. Great leadership shines a light that can invigorate or rejuvenate. Great leadership can wipe away today's pain or panic by focusing efforts toward a better tomorrow. Great leadership can bend steel. Hardened hearts that have been hammered to steel by heartbreak are pried open with great leadership. *Great leaders get more sugar (money, power, respect, better jobs) because they bring forth the best chance to achieve success from plans, hopes, and dreams.*

Truthfully, not all companies want their managers to be great leaders—it depends on the leadership of the company—and not all managers can be great leaders. Some managers might outright dismiss the extra effort and awareness that is required to realize the ultimate combo-platter. But take a moment and think of the scope of your hospitality/service management job. It likely includes driving sales; controlling costs; meeting or exceeding standards; doling out rewards and punishments; communicating up, down, and across; and serving and protecting the organization, among other things. As such, you need to be part shaman-ambassador-coach-maintenance worker-camp counselor-traffic cop, or better yet, all leader-manager. I prefer the term *leadager,* an excellent manager who is an excellent leader, further detailed as not one at the expense of the other but doing both well. As a *leadager,* you will be practicing the fine art (or is it a science?) of *managementship*, the highly sought, seldom natural, combination of great management and leadership (best viewed with an old-world sensibility toward craftsmanship or apprenticeship). By comparison, if the "real" job of acting can be considered a "noble craft" then by all rights we must include the job of "running" a real business within the same realm.

Meeting topics:

- What makes a great manager or leader?
- What makes a great manager or leader?
- What are the top 5 things a leader must do?
- What are the top 5 things a manager must do? (Helpful hint: Now you have a top ten daily to-do list.)
- Is *managementship* a tradecraft?
- What professional characteristics need to be "out in front" and thereby, increasing your chances to cultivate a successful tribe?
- Are you "home-growing" these characteristics?

Business management gurus of the world have long stated that most business managers have leadership built into their job description. Natural-born leaders will need to be skilled at actually managing business operations if they hope to be successful in a managerial position. Business realities dictate that if you are named to head a department or group, you are expected to lead its direction, manage the resources, and be accountable for results, good or bad (people, performance, profits, culture, legacy, and so on).

So there you have it. I advocate combining leader and manager to illustrate the point that if you are managing people, it is the proper terminology to use. Even though most old school folks will never make a job title out of any part of the word leadership, the fact remains that management and leadership are logistically inseparable. If you desire to be a great *leadager* (remember, "gets more sugar…") you will internalize and sanctify this union (speak now or forever hold your piece… of pizza).

Chapter 2
Make More Dough

There is a common theme among managers in the hospitality/service organization setting. Faster than most would imagine, a single, career-related question becomes uppermost in one's mind. The million-dollar question inevitably becomes, "How can I make more money?"

Here is my take on the most common paths to wealth enhancement. If you have an abundance of skills and talent, or you are an entrepreneur at heart, start and run your own successful business (unsuccessful ones don't pay very well). In lieu of that, however, if you are seeking a substantial increase in your pay, it is most practical to develop *leadager* skills that are highly valued by the people who provide the high-paying jobs. The goal should be to create an intersection between what they desire and what you can deliver. (Please note that this differs greatly from the common rift between parents and their children...a declaration of childish wants, closely followed by tantrums when satisfaction is deemed to be not immediate enough.)

"Success is not rare—it is common.... It is a matter of adjusting one's efforts to obstacles and one's abilities to a service needed by others. There is no other possible success. But most people think of it in terms of getting; success, however, begins in terms of giving."—Henry Ford, Sr.

MONEY-MAKIN' MOXIE

I maintain that there are seven capabilities in our industry where, at all levels, the demand outstrips the supply. (Relax, *mon ami;* none of them requires a college degree.) You are not guaranteed anything, particularly not fame and fortune, but if you strengthen your capabilities in the following areas, you will exponentially increase your value in the world of work, or *WOW* (oh yeah, in real life, too). The following lists the leadership craft—the moxie—that should be paralleling your "hard skills" management development.

1. Increase your value by being a trustee. From hard-knock experience, all kinds of institutions—from businesses to prisons—have had to develop trustee systems, or key carriers, as a necessary support structure. Despite any gray areas of morality one could argue, most people know what trust means to them and generally speaking, the world seeks ethical people in whom we can trust.

Valueless, directionless, or moral-mess employees wreak havoc on an organization. If they happen to occupy a leadership position, it can be a death sentence for the company. Although individual perceptions of "big" or "small" infractions can vary greatly, unethical behavior must have consequences, regardless of the size of the violation. I'm talking about more than the preferred traits that prevent lying, cheating, and stealing. This also goes beyond being one of the "good ones," dependably looking out for the company's interests and reliably and consistently working hard.

What is truly ethical does not fall into a gray area. Over time, we all experience the variety of ways people define trust and subsequent expectations. Trust in this context is a broadened definition of character. It is not just what is in your mind or heart; it is entering the fray, consistently coming through and doing the right thing.

The following is my general rule of thumb: As a trustee, your involvement doesn't make things worse; optimally, your involvement always makes things measurably better (with no threat of prison, besmirched reputations, insolvency, or residual skeletons left in the closet). *Can you be trusted to make things better? Much better?*

2. Increase your value by being a GOAT. Do you follow through from "say" to "do"? (Hey, that's catchy.) Passion can fuel a certain type of frenetic energy and perseverance, but business is a never-ending marathon of what's next, and some people just don't have the makeup to go the distance once the excitement wanes. Determination is good, but accomplishment is tops.

The discipline that is required to stick to a commitment—nay, *attack* commitments—in spite of distractions or pitfalls, is rare air indeed. But this is not about the woefully under-aware, blind loyalists. This, *mi amigo,* is the art of GOATS, which means Go Over Around or Through Stuff (or your "s" word of choice) to meet objectives. *As* GOATS *you have the ability to get things done. Even more important, though, is whether you can get more things done right more often than most other people.*

3. Increase your value by being a catalyst. Can you guide diverse groups of people into positively aligned relationships? In your *WOW* this might be called managing, supervising, coordinating, organizing, leading, or baby-sitting. Whatever it's called, the broad yet decisive test is not whether you know what to do, but rather, will people follow you when you do it? What is your *people-pull* quotient?

If you are running a single sidewalk kiosk, then you only have to answer to yourself. But if even one person reports to you, it is important to assess whether you have done enough by asking yourself the following question: *Am I worth following?* (Do you know what you're doing? Do you help others to succeed? Can they count on you to do the right thing? Do you set a clear path for victory?)

To get to the bottom of the answers to these questions, ask yourself how credible, influential, impactful, or trustworthy you would be without the authority of your position (your title at work). Could you achieve the same buy-in results without your title and positional authority? *Never* underestimate the major role positive relationships play in determining business success. *Whether it is uniting the tribe, the team, or the neighbors, the value of being able to bring people together to achieve collective goals is indisputable. Are you a practiced and proven catalyst?*

4. Increase your value by being a translator. Knowing more than one language in a global economy is a highly valued trait. In fact, certain American domestic demographic subsets could use translators (e.g., North vs. South, East Coast vs. Left Coast, young vs. old). However, I'm referring to the ability to distill matters to their essence and then communicate the message to other people in such a way that they can easily grasp and respond. *Can you gain and retain attention in a world filled with distraction? Can you bring simplification to a society of clutter? After your interpretation and translation, do meaning and motivation resonate with your intended audience?*

You might hone your knack for speaking, writing, or visual arts and parlay that into a marketing, research, or design contribution. I suppose to some degree the simple act of being heard or seen does count, although a high number of people would describe the pinnacle of translation success to be the achievement of "buy in." The *true* success in this area is measured by a close connection to a desired response—say, if participation, traffic, sales, productivity, and profitability are all up.

Can you fly a flag that other people will rally around? Do you inspire others to go that extra distance? Does your "translation" of directions and destinations provoke stellar performance?

5. Increase your value by being a sunshine-maker. You have heard the terms rainmaker, playmaker, dealmaker, moneymaker, and kingmaker. For slang language to work itself into everyday usage, it often carries a significant substantive implication rather than just being the latest fringe trend. In the case of the sunshine-maker, it is a highly prized professional designation.

Every business has cold, cloudy days. Traffic, sales, or profits did not materialize. A competitor steps up their game, a prized employee leaves. The economy tanks and the bank line of credit gets canceled. There is a food-source scare or a flu panic. In the face of ever-changing business climates, at the end of the day, it will still be about achieving desired results.

Enter the sunshine-maker, casting away the external clouds, mustering resolve, realigning resources, and regaining momentum. They bring the right kind of heat and enthusiasm from above.

In my experience the more people you know beyond hello, the better the chance you will be able to enlist some help for your challenge. It never hurts to be good at what you do but let's face it: Business is a numbers game. The more people you can count on (including yourself), the greater your chance for success. Do you make a mark by drawing from your personal resources—contacts, charisma, cleverness, and connections—to move the business along substantially in a positive direction (also known as driving the top and bottom lines)?

Do you have the ability to use your business mojo to pump things up?

A real business sunshine-maker will make good things happen (let it shine, let it shine) and will do it legally and ethically. Can you? Will you?

6. Increase your value by being a business mechanic. This is best defined as finding answers and solutions that resolve other people's problems. If your car is not running right, you take it to the shop or if you have the right tools, maybe fix it yourself—and so it goes for a business. Difficult situations can require different personnel, as well as a mindset shift to reverse a trend or find a solution. As business fortunes ebb and flow, there are boundless opportunities to provide both micro and macro assistance.

Becoming a specialist or an expert is the fastest route to the mechanic title. Some people specialize in a specific business function, such as finance, information technology, human resources, marketing, operations, sales, or supply chain. Others make careers out of turnarounds or roll-outs. Then there are those who strive to be well-rounded across all of the various functional areas of business, better preparing themselves for the roles of multi-unit manager, president, or CEO.

Take note. Becoming a troubleshooting mechanic means you will be involved in more stressful, higher-risk/higher-reward situations. *In order for these types of opportunities to present themselves, your ability and track record as a mechanic must be so pronounced and proven that you separate yourself from the rest of the pack. You are no longer one of the "I think I cans." When you hear the engine knocking, you can make the right call without lifting the hood.*

7. Increase your value by becoming a shepherd. Staying plugged into trends and popular culture can be a challenge for some business people. There is always a market for knowledgeable trend watchers, idea generators/incubators, skillful borrowers, and repackagers.

Pretend for a moment that you have set up a new shop; let's call it "Out Think, Inc." You are in the business of invention, imagination, and ingenuity. Here is the kicker: You must develop many ideas to produce one killer brainchild, and it can take numerous attempts to bring an idea through the planning and execution phases before a successful outcome can be realized. Creative thinkers, idea generators, and inventors can change the fortune of a company, but bad ideas can ruin one. A string of smaller, easy-to-execute ideas can be viewed as keeping a business topically evergreen and relevant. Shepherds utilize their imaginations to bring inspiration into their jobs (injecting a WOW! into the "world of work").

However, the real unmet need lies in the capability to recognize a good idea, generated from anywhere, and then move it from the drawing board to a trial test and beyond. *It takes a shepherd to nurture, care-take or protect an idea, and then usher a mental effort into something that makes a difference. Are you a competent and committed shepherd?*

Trustee, GOAT, catalyst, translator, sunshine-maker, mechanic, and *shepherd* are all mantles given to people who have the ability to move a business in the right direction. In an era filled with so many undesirable stereotypes, here are a few labels to which one can aspire that actually will separate you from the pack.

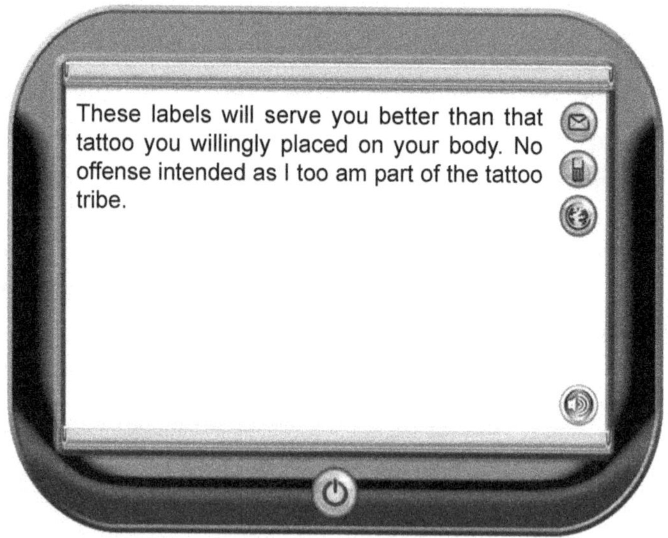

If you can lead in areas others can't or won't, you enhance your chances to be valued beyond the job title of manager. If you are able to answer the call when your organization is seeking to fill their needs, you move to the front of the next money line.

Some of the above may be "too far down the road" for you. You are looking for the shortcut to more money now. Sorry, it really doesn't work that way. You must have skills, be good at something, and be recognized as such before anything super-good starts to flow back to you. There won't be much of a chance to be a *great* leader or manager unless first and foremost you are a *good* one (run before you fly…).

MONEY-MAKIN' SKILLS

Over the years, I have been hounded by tribemates looking for a raise in pay (not unwarranted, but alas, still pervasive). If you want a pay increase to materialize at a faster pace, you must do some homework in addition to your work duties. What follows is the *hospitality-specific* response I have given to those on the money hunt: Whenever you are being evaluated for hiring, a promotion, or a raise, start with the most significant accomplishments you can cite from your recent professional history. It is both the *wide* and the *narrow* definitions of success that will define your evaluation.

What was your specific involvement in achieving strong results, forwarding programs, changing the business climate, and so forth? What were the scope and the scale of your responsibilities? What was your total staff size, including direct reports? Did you have P&L responsibility? What was the size of your budget? Be prepared to quickly and crisply articulate your business results, not just your activities.

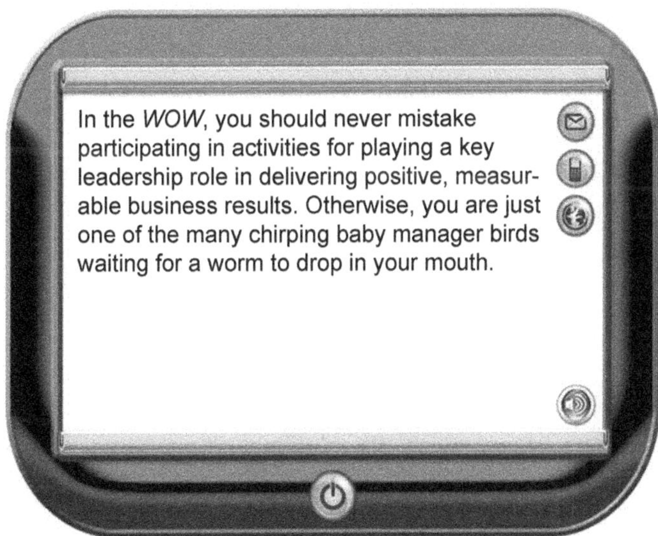

Itemizing a track record of your successes is the easiest way for the *powers that be* to evaluate and elevate you to greater responsibility, and *hello,* "mad stacks, jack!" Regardless of how well you have performed, seeking more money in the same role might provide incremental increases, but eventually you will slam into a hard salary ceiling. Most organizations usually calculate compensation packages based on titles or responsibility levels and pay grades. Rarely can you break beyond the pre-set ranges.

You must work, plan, dream, and scheme your way to bigger jobs (of course, only through honest and ethical schemes). This is the most direct route to pay raises significant enough to really upgrade your lifestyle. The simple fact is that all persons of the same *leadager* level or title are in a competition for the next opportunity, whether they buy into it, act above it, care about it or not. (Everybody sing: "It's a dog-eat-dog world…")

Assuming your performance earns you the right to get your hat thrown into the ring for a promotion, the next assessment hurdles you face are those of *pace and progression.* Never underestimate the positive effect on your wallet the aggressive pursuit of advancement brings. The death-knell for anyone seeking advancement is having the same level of experience without a promotion for five-plus years. You will then be deemed as not promotable, a poor career manager, and/or lacking drive or talent. Hiring managers will be wary of you. ("If you can't do it for yourself, how will you do it for us?")

If you were to ask a group of assistant managers to cite the major hurdles standing between them and more money, you would quite likely hear the following typical excuses (always someone else's fault):

"The company says there aren't any opportunities right now."
"They say I don't have the right experience."
"My supervisor hassles me all the time."
"I've got a bad team; they're holding me back."
"I didn't go far enough in skool."
"They like Joe/Jill better than me."

If you were to ask a collection of *leadagers* what major issues they consistently assess when deciding to promote someone, you might hear the following:

- Poor transition from an hourly to salary mentality
- Questionable integrity
- Inconsistent follow-up/follow-through on projects
- Denial of accountability

- Lacking initiative
- Poor judgment
- Weak interpersonal skills
- Poor financial acumen/performance

Ah, here's a light-bulb moment for you: All of it is deemed to be within your control.

The perspective gap between these two groups is real, and it exists in some form or another in every workplace. The common complaint of my peers who provide the advancement opportunity is not, "Why is this C player acting like a C player?" but rather, "Why is this potential A player content to settle for B or C level performance? What is wrong with him/her?"

There are many ways to assess/measure success and progression, and you likely will have your job performance reviewed by a multitude of methods. It is *irrefutably important,* however, for you to ask for, listen to, and act on the feedback provided to you by the organization, your peers, and your tribe. This should not be limited to formal review periods or self-esteem firing squads; keep your eyes and ears open to what people think of your performance. It's just like wetting your finger and sticking it in the air to check which way the wind is blowing.

It is also of *equal importance* to measure how you are doing through your own eyes, a self-review by utilizing a progress chart/review form of your own design. This serves you in many ways:

1. You will appear ultraprepared at the time of your performance review by presenting the facts rather than relying on a "taxed to the max" memory—either yours or theirs—and hopefully, it will preclude a one-sided information dump.
2. You can work on developmental opportunities (fix weaknesses) before review periods are concluded. Your willingness and ability to take an identified weakness and turn it into a strength is a sign of executive level potential. *It is eye-poppingly positive to have the self-awareness to identify and pursue professional betterment without prompting.*
3. You can track your accomplishments and benchmarks for personal development in the context of moving closer to your dream job (which may or may not be a vision your current employer shares with you).

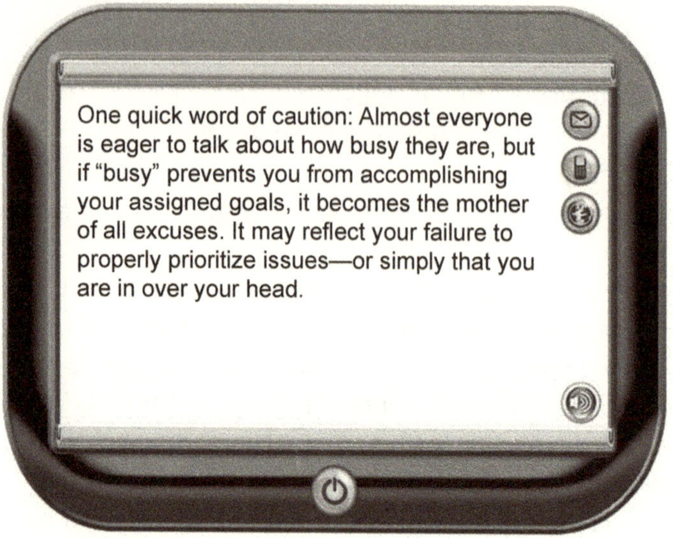

4. You will have up-to-date details for your resume should you need it.

PRE-REVIEW WORKSHEET

The point of this exercise is to force yourself into thinking about and acting on the pursuit of accomplishments. At the end of every quarter, or semiannually at a minimum, use this as a framework to detail accomplishments, that is, *measurable results, targeted benchmarks,* and *key areas of concern.* This "business speak" is really the only language your reviewer cares about.

Review the ways in which your leadership-by-example and role-model style have personally contributed to the organization's success by positively influencing the guests and your tribemates through the professional example you have consistently set. Are you positively using your influence and authority to induce others to follow your lead toward betterment of the entire operation?

____

____

In what ways did your personal efforts positively affect the operation's profitability? Did you create/utilize systems that reduced expenses, maximized resources, and/or exceeded financial expectations?

____

____

Describe your personal effort and impact on improving the quality of the products, operational performance, and workplace culture/environment.

____

____

Comment on your contribution to developing the skills of others through your mentoring, guidance, and ability to seek and keep A-plus players/tribemates. Include your assessments, adaptation/advancement of systems, supportive partnership behavior, training, and motivation that enabled tribemates to contribute to overall/individual goals. (Also, who in the heck did you make ready for promotion?)

____

____

How have you improved your knowledge and skill level since your last review? How have you specifically increased your value as a professional?

____

____

Review your specific accomplishments toward minimizing liability exposure for the organization, including but not limited to liquor license, health department, fire department, workers compensation, harassment issues, cash security, and accidents.

____

____

How have you positively affected the proactive maintenance or repairs of equipment and the daily cleanliness of the operation?

____

____

After reminiscing about my own experiences on completion of the above worksheet, I decided to reinforce the common mantra that so many hospitality/service companies wish their young managers would embrace: Take hold! It is a privilege for a company to entrust to you a multimillion-dollar asset for safe-keeping. At the same time, this same company is making it possible for you to develop personally and professionally, to enhance your professional reputation, to increase your personal wealth, and to guide the development of others. Do not take this privilege lightly. There are "hidden" opportunities and benefits that accompany a *managementship* position; take advantage of them. (*If you do good, you can do well.*)

Meeting topics:

- Do you have ambition?
- What's your plan to make more money for yourself?
- In addition to the hard skills necessary to succeed in your job, what kind of moxie is important?
- Do you know the difference between activities and accomplishments?
- Why are pace and progression important if you have ambition?
- Identify the major issues that prevent a person from being promoted.
- Do you track your own career progress with a measurement system of your own design?

Chapter 3

Blood Bound: My Start

Oh sure, I had previously dabbled in the typical early teen jobs—mowing lawns, pumping gas, and selling fireworks. But it was on the eve of my sixteenth birthday that a "Help Wanted" sign on the door of the nearby fern-and-brass steakhouse beckoned to me. My underutilized adolescent logic kicked in: "Hey, I could ride my bike to work there—perfect!" My plan was to lollygag through the first half of the summer by working part-time. This would allow me to bank some moola before I turned sixteen, thus claiming my young American freedom pass: a driver's license.

The main claim to fame of this particular steakhouse was an artichoke side dish and an all-you-can-eat salad bar. Ah...the seventies. I was the poster child for chump-rookies in this, my first "real job," and to prove the point, I was smacked right in my fifteen-year-old kisser with unrelenting chaos and a drive-by cast of deeply crazed characters.

The owner/manager was an overweight, undersexed (I'm only guessing at this) screamer. I also recall many long-faced, anger-laced servers and a steady stream of bottle-blonde, cigarette-smoking cocktail waitresses who eagerly engaged in overly dramatic verbal bouts with the boss.

Our kitchen manager was a part-time dope smoker (his prideful boast) and full-time lady-slayer. His long, blond, surfer-dude hair was always in a ponytail, rebelliously dangling down the middle of his back. He wore his "old soul" middle-twenties like a cloak of unyielding coolness.

Understaffed and overpressured, this motley crew's daily goal was to survive the shift and get to the party (some things change, some stay the same), a gathering that held court nightly in a succession of apartments and basements throughout the metro area. I can recall unfailingly stereotypic mid-to-late-seventies iconography—Frye boots, Angel Flight pants, Nic-Nic shirts, lava lamps, bong water, gold-plated medallions, aviator sunglasses, and jug wine.

I would not go so far as to say that I never inhaled, but thanks to some youthful missteps that resulted in massive hurls, I had come hardwired with intake limits on sin-taxed items.

Initially, I was hired as a day-shift busser at the aforementioned steak place. While I enjoyed the tip-sharing aspect of the job, I hated the spit-out half-chewed steak fat cleverly hidden in napkins, crushed cigarette butts mashed into baked potatoes, and tiny pools of baby spit-up my fingers inevitably slid into as I cleared the platters. *Really* hated all of it.

Expediently, my untrained digits would find their way deep into all manner of coffee cups and water glasses, four to six at a time, in an effort to minimize my trips to the dish pit. Then, my hands covered with enough DNA to keep a crime lab busy for six months, I would immediately grab clean silverware and napkins for new table set-ups, completely ignorant of even the most basic aspects of food safety or sanitation. As I look back, I am certain that the only time soap touched my hands was for a good post-shift clean-up on my way out the door.

The owner/manager had defined success for us, the faceless bussers, as the speed by which we hauled stuff away without dropping anything—and how fast we carried stuff back. His secondary concerns were whether we would show up on time, work later than scheduled, and pick up extra shifts "under the table" (i.e., "off the books") so he could avoid paying us overtime.

This same guy will forever be etched into my gray matter as the crass man who flogged one particular crude word into practically every sentence. Whenever he thought anyone was not working hard enough, which was *always*, he would slur the statement, "Quit your dickin' around." Or the ever-present inane questions, "Are they dickin' around?" and "Who's dickin' around in there?" As you might imagine, a young staff routinely fed this steady diet of "quirky-bird" soon began sending forth wickedly scalding impersonations of said crass man whenever he exited the room.

In hindsight, what was most notable about this not-too-atypical restaurant experience was any semblance of real training. The "Hoss Boss" did not take any time to reinforce the importance of guest expectations and satisfaction. Ah, the old school...*sink or swim, baby*! We learned the job from the folks who were doing the job, for better or worse.

"You're too...slow, simple, and stooopid" were the oft-repeated laments about my various shortcomings. Coupled with my limited work experience, this created for me a feeling of perpetual failure. *Leadagers* take note: When developing talent, the negative pictures you paint or suggestions you plant have a good chance to wreak havoc on the young and inexperienced or those with self-esteem challenges. Treat people the way you wish for them to be or cut the cord quickly. Less suffering is better overall for both sides.

I quickly became completely disenchanted with *el jefe*'s delivery and the front of the house's ongoing soap opera. The kitchen, on the other hand, had intrigued me from the very beginning. Led by the "rebel prince," it was like a medieval alchemist shop—raw food dollied into the back door, followed by *bang-clang-boom*, a cacophony of guttural barks, a trailing twist of smoke, then, *voilà!* Beautifully prepared meals appeared in the expo window. Like most folks who are too young to serve cocktails, I cajoled and connived to pick up any and all kitchen shifts in an effort to join the "real action."

"Okay, on Sunday you can bust suds." I still remember basking in the glory of those words. Despite flying straight into my well-established disgust and borderline phobia of spittle-laden leavings, for the first time, I became professionally goal-driven.

Here was the plan: Perform well enough at washing dishes to be noticed, and then work that into a better job in the kitchen. Subsequently, after proving myself committed to working quickly and until the work was done, coupled with a flexible willingness either to run my mouth or shut it down as the situation warranted, I was promoted to a prep cook position.

Prepping food was a produce-or-you-will-be-barked-at proposition: washing and cutting lettuce for the salad bar; trimming chicken and cubing steak for teriyaki skewers; cracking frozen lobster tails and slathering butter, spices and plastic wrap over the top. Measure that, mix this, but mostly, quickness was demanded.

This little kitchen had to be the point of origin for the term *breakneck speed.* Again, this was "old school" and there were tons of accidents. Never was there a mention of proper lifting techniques and nary a rubber glove in sight. Cuts and burns in that kitchen were an hourly occurrence. We had more bandages and burn ointment "on the fly" than "remake" dinners. Most of my kitchen hits and nicks were inconsequential—until I was *stabbed.*

The culprit was waiting for my arrival—a stiletto-thin, serrated steak knife with evil intent. Like a viper on the trail, this bad boy was blade up in the recesses of the only rubber mat in the kitchen. It had been dropped, walked on, and wedged into place by the numb shoes of my fellow workers. One busy evening while diligently applying my adopted value of "speed above all," I dashed to the front of the dish pit, my vision blocked at the waist by a bus tub full of dirty tools.

As my right foot came to a harried stop, it pressed securely down on the mat-trapped handle of the knife, leveraging the blade tip up at an angle that allowed it to rip itself through the thin canvas of my ratty tennis shoe and then into the inside meat of my late-arriving left foot. I mean, I *buried* that knife in there. This was real pain, not a schoolyard scrape, and it is here, I confess, that the only thing that kept me from screaming like a scared five-year-old was the swift reaction of the battle-tested kitchen veterans. The alarm was sounded by the first amigo to see me and then, "Wha' the f'enheimer did choo *do?"* said the big dawg kitchen manager.

A knife was protruding from the side of my foot like the curb antenna on my grandpa's Chevy, but what should I do? Yell? Jerk it out? Or just continue to hold my breath and spastically hop around? I know now that my lapsed reaction was because of pure shock, but I did not have long to process the event.

Two or three white-apron blurs grabbed me and together we three-legged-raced to the three-compartment sink. They lifted my leg onto the side of the stainless steel tank. I became woozy. "We gotta take it out and look at it," they barked.

"Okay," I feebly replied. I shouldn't have looked. There against the silver sink was my dangling bloody foot. I saw the hand grab the knife and tug. It hurt coming out, but it was my flesh entrails and the flow of deep red color that I so vividly remember. My tennis shoe and sock were off a moment later and the cold water was cascading over my bare foot. The full blast torrent barely diluted my burgundy-colored blood swirling at the bottom of the sink. Then, first aid goo, gauze, duct tape, and an ice bag, followed by momentary humanity.

After my patch-up, while sitting on an over-turned ice bucket, the kitchen manager came over to me and said, "Dude, that's bad. You gotta go to the doc."

I said weakly, "My car's got a stick. I don't think I can work the clutch."

"That's okay, I'll drive ya."

"But what about the dinner rush?" I asked.

"I'll get Bobo [his second in command] to run the line. Let's go!"

I received support and attention not from the "boss/owner" who was "tsk-tsking" in the background, but from our *recognized* tribal leader: the kitchen manager. This leader didn't give a hoot about arti-"chokes" or potato-"bakers" when it got real. He stepped up and personally ensured my well-being when it counted the most. To recap in a nutshell: I got a tetanus shot, stitches, and time off.

When I returned to work, I was part of the cultural lore. The kitchen crew all blamed some pond-scum sucker from the front of the house for being lazy (okay, some disharmonious comments may have emanated from me) and causing this wounding of "one of us."

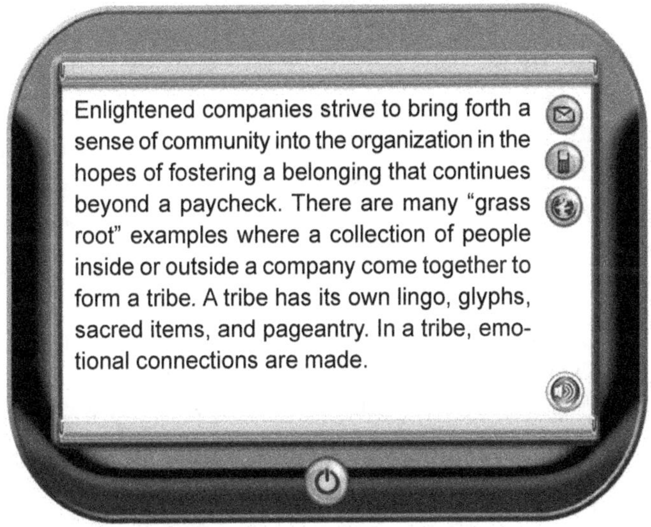

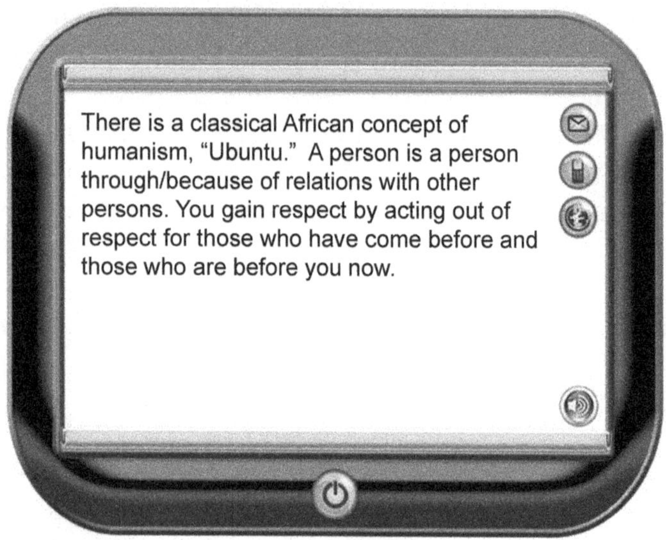

One of us. Yes, by working hard before the bloodletting, by not fainting at the sight of my gored foot, and by returning to work, I had made my "bones." I even picked up a nickname, "Blood" (as in copious amounts of), long before there was any gang member connotation.

Like many "hourly workers" before and after, I started that summer just trying to get a job and ended it by taking a wild ride with the kitchen tribe.

Any job, even a great one, can only provide a monetary connection and fleeting "perks." The closer you get to tribal relations with members caring and connecting to each other on an emotional level, the sharper you make your competitive spear.

This highlights the need for strong cultural values and strong *leadagers* who will go and show the way.

Meeting topics:

- Describe your best and worst days/nights at work. What did you learn from the extremes?
- What do you do differently now in order to increase the good/diminish the bad?
- How do you build tribal ties in your group?
- What are your favorite "'round the campfire" stories that advance the culture or performance of your group?
- How are you identifying the future/current leaders of the group? What are the criteria, what are the rewards?

CHAPTER 4

YOUR START: YOUR CHOICE

MANAGEMENT AND LEADERSHIP ARE IN NO small part about meeting and/or exceeding accountability and responsibility levels and established goals. It takes real effort to be a success.

Let's pretend that somebody, somewhere, has just taken out the manager-makin' magic wand, pinged you on the head, and declared you, henceforth, to be known as *manager*. My friend, you have now left the hourly ranks and stepped into a different realm. The transition from solo work responsibility—aka individual contributor—into the care and feeding of a tribe that has been assigned to you is a very different type of exercise. As you attempt to enlist, execute, organize, and prioritize, you may very well be dumbstruck by the depth of the muck you must rake.

If you assume management responsibilities relatively early in your career, you may also face an internal struggle. Contrary to the common misconception held by some in our society, immaturity, irresponsibility, and youth are not synonymous. However, it does seem to be increasingly rare that an individual with little responsibility outside of work suddenly successfully voodoos him- or herself into a conscientious and responsible superstar employee. Like it or not, most savvy employers use past behavior as the basis for predicting future behavior.

Will you be the one to grab the joystick and do what it takes to meet (and exceed) your new "uber" responsibilities? Or will you cling to the stereotypes of irresponsibility (the *I'm only doing this for a while* approach, the *fun-first* mantra, the *don't-dog-me* attitude) only to trek defiantly into professional mediocrity?

If you have decided to "do what it takes," keep in mind that whoever hired or promoted you wants you to make *themselves* look good—it is in their best interest. Sure, they might offer a veneer of interest in your happiness, but basically, they are hoping for some help and a few home runs (or you would not have been hired). Additionally, they'd like to be known for having a keen eye for talent. Stay aware of their self-interest and proactively attempt to extract from him/her an initial picture of how success is defined within the organization. If you triangulate this first-blush picture with what the top bosses are currently "incentivizing" and what your direct supervisor is prioritizing, you will begin to understand what success means and what "doing a good job" entails—a solid starting point for your efforts.

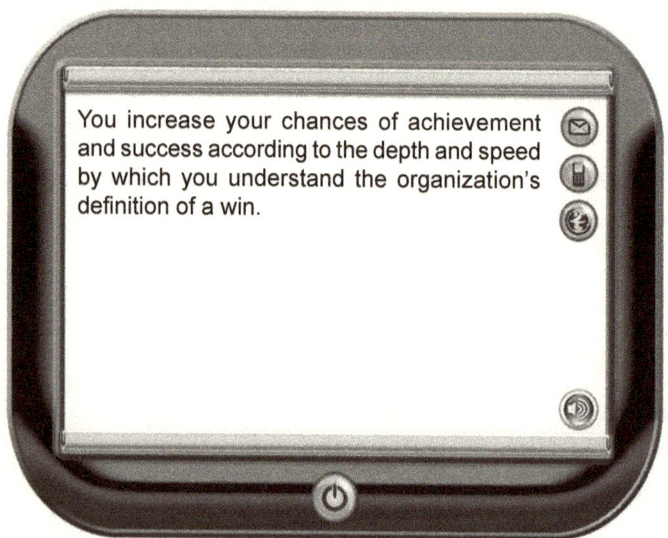

If you are a freshly minted manager, you don't have much experience, but you likely have ample time to devote to your job. This is one of the reasons time is referred to as money—as in, if you use your time wisely, you can earn more money.

As careers and people mature, most folks aspire to accumulate more things, and as this happens, there usually are more demands on your time. Consider the transition from Spartan single life to couplehood and beyond—serious dating, a better car, marriage, dream vacations, a baby or two, a new house, finishing off the basement in time for your elderly in-law to move in with you. All of these milestones require some level of participation on your part and all carry the potential to diminish the amount of time you will devote to work. This requires that most senior managers excel at *plate spinning*, i.e., multitasking, to deliver ever-increasing levels of productivity.

You, on the other hand (if you are able to put down the remote, the mouse, the cell phone, or any glass pipe), can devote some serious focus and energy to becoming a manager *par excellence* ahead of schedule and expectations. This devotion to the tasks at hand will arm you with a clear competitive advantage over your peers. The key is that you must resoundingly refuse to allow your personal habits to sidetrack you professionally.

Regardless of how long you have been in the industry, as you ascend to manager, there will be a dynamic, semi-seismic shift in the intensity and variety of demands placed on you. Don't make the mistake of thinking that because you have observed other people doing "the management thing" that you know all there is to know. At this point you have no idea what you don't know. When you are charged with driving yourself and others toward business success, much goes on that a casual onlooker might miss.

Speaking of driving, consider this new challenge analogous to what you faced when learning how to drive a car. Do you remember how little attention you paid as a child when the driving duties were being handled by someone else? (Seemed sorta easy to get from here to there, didn't it?) Soon, your interest and participation were piqued as the reality of doing it yourself loomed on the horizon. Finally, after months of practice for some, years for others, good driving skills were, hopefully, the end result.

For managers and for drivers, the repeated exposure to different elements, situations, and conditions serves to broaden and hone skills; you will soon see the business equivalent of driving in snow, rain, and mountains, as well as parallel parking in the big city. While we are in the midst of this particular driving analogy, try to remember that skilled, safe driving requires that most of your attention be focused forward and sideways with a few quick glances into the rearview mirror (scan, scan, scan). Similarly, driving forward a successful career calls for the same habitual, broad—yet selective—vision.

It has been a frequent task of mine to remind many individuals that whatever transpired when they were five years old, a sophomore in college, or in their last job does not have to continue to be a distracting force in their current work life (i.e., attempting to drive forward while staring in the rearview mirror).

Of course, we all have had negative experiences in our lives, but it is seriously unhealthy to use them as an excuse or barrier that precludes any future *redefining* moments. Carrying this load of extra baggage is truly burdensome when attempting to learn new skills. Bad things have happened to all of us, yet no matter what you've endured, someone else has had it worse. If you choose to share your laments with others, the nice people of this Earth may sympathize or even help you out, but the primary response you'll receive in the world of work (*WOW*) will be, "So, are you still able to carry your assigned share of the workload?" and more likely, "Can you pull more than your load or weight?" This is also known as "picking up the slack."

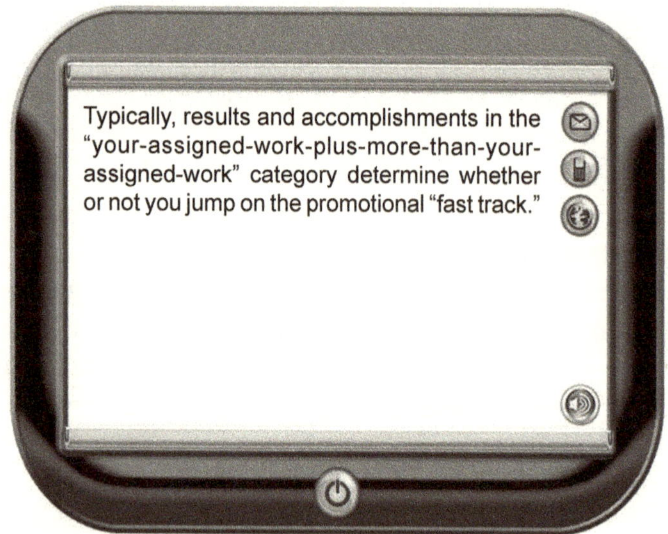

Obviously, I am disregarding nepotism, throwing somebody else under the bus, or any other shortcuts you may attempt to leverage on your way up. The above is simply the unsweetened truth and the origin of the business motto, "more-better-faster." Bottom line: Do your best to muster up a continuous effort that prevents your own personal dramas from entering, tainting, or disrupting the workplace. Your career will thank you. (If you *must* add drama, head to Hollywood!)

MANAGEMENTSHIP

Upon assuming a new job with heightened levels of responsibility, many people may experience anxiety and frustration. These feelings are normal. They can actually serve you well, so it is a mistake to completely quell them. They do diminish on their own, but that's later, much later. The resulting keenness—the edge this discomfort brings—should serve to sharpen your focus. And as stated above, a sharp focus is your friend.

You will also serve yourself well by quickly developing relationships with people in every department and level of the company—to the extent that is practical—to garner knowledge and wisdom from different perspectives. Trust me, the senior-most levels do not have a lock on all available knowledge and "smarts" in the company and the wise ones know this.

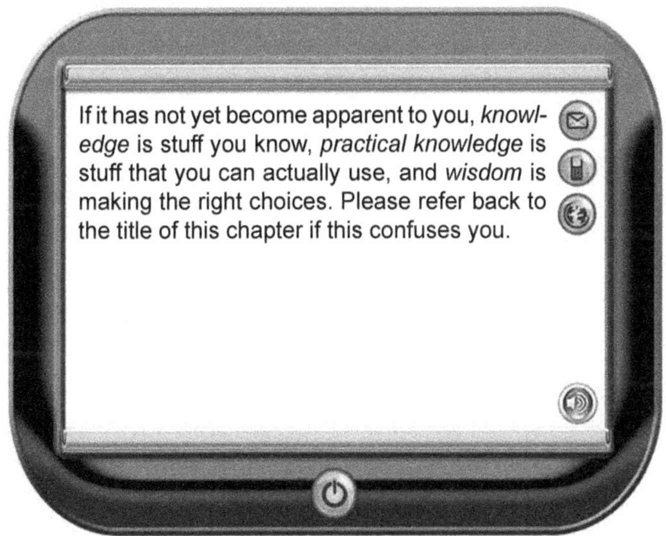

Make the right choice early on in your career to work toward becoming a *leadager*, not just another manager. Most people ascend to the top (highest paying) jobs in our industry by becoming good or great at doing the various jobs over which they will eventually have supervision. A few have singular talent that outshines the rest. Some have a way to build relationships that are more successful than most with the teams they are asked to supervise. Most are hardworking leaders who have a great grasp of managing the details. As stated before, when leadership and management come together it is *managementship*. I submit that the mastery of this craft is as lofty or worthy a goal as any.

Meeting topics:

- What are the big choices facing you when you accept a management position?
- How does your group define "win"? Do the tribemates with the greatest guest contact share this definition?
- Why is broad, yet selective vision important to a leadager?
- How do you define the differences between knowledge and wisdom?
- What is the one competitive advantage that comes from being placed in stressful situations?
- Do you view managementship a tradecraft? If yes, are you setting your sights on becoming a mastercraftsperson?

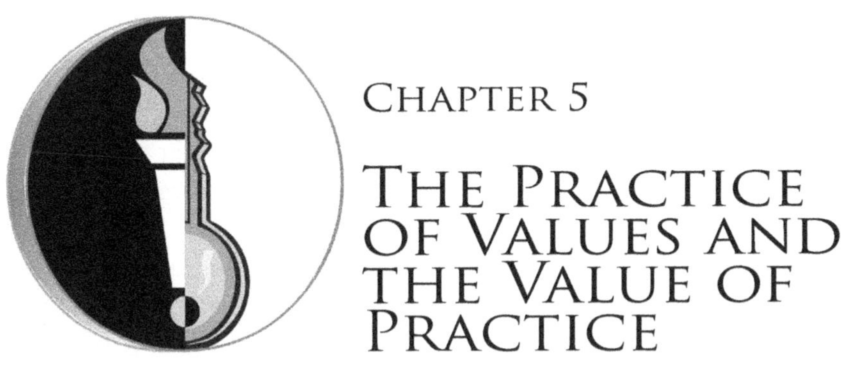

Chapter 5

The Practice of Values and the Value of Practice

"Less energy on emotions, more energy on solutions" is a useful perspective most *employers* would like all of their *employees* to *employ.* Clutch performers, whether they are on a battlefield, sporting field, or world stage, all have a rare trait: the ability to do what the moment requires. If you have grace under fire, if you are calm under pressure and in the end come through, it is majestically magnetic. Some might suggest this is merely poise or temperament. I call it leading by example and it is hard to do. This rare ability to gather oneself, draw from and apply all that is required to meet and conquer challenges, is actually impossibly hard to accomplish when you're flooded with unbridled emotions. In your role as a *leadager*, it is far better to be the eye of the storm that surrounds you. (Too zen?) Okay then, try this: If you're "going nuts" when things are going crazy, you're teaching nuts behavior!

The above mindset should also be coupled with the perspective that almost all necessary management and leadership skills are improved with practice. Be diligent over time about adding to your skills. Try to be as dedicated as you were when you collected comic books, downloads, dolls, or trading cards. Also, be humble and be accepting of the mistakes that will inevitably accompany your learning curve. This can be difficult, especially if you were a strong hourly employee. Sniff, sniff...smell that? That's the scent of the easily awakened fear that resides within most adults, the fear of looking bad or dumb. Try to ignore this fear for the greater good of your (hopefully) long career.

SKILL-BUILDING BY IMMERSION

Most "top dogs" expect you to have a hiccup or two early on. If not, they are being unreasonable and unrealistic—unless of course, you are ordering hours of porn on their dime while staying at the training facility. (Yes, a newly hired manager staying at the motel next to the training store I was in charge of really did that!) Continue to practice building your skills. Throw yourself into the things you are afraid of or haven't done before, regardless of how you look. Practice on the P.O.S. (cash register), run food, make drinks, work on the line, check IDs, break down, clean up—anything you're not comfortable with. Do not try to "just get through it." Remember, your professional development will become a part-time endeavor once you are given full-time responsibilities. A sense of urgency on your part as it relates to acquiring new skills will be noticed and viewed as a real positive.

Take advantage of this "early learner" period by asking many questions. It is far better to be a super-curious wing-nut who reduces mistakes as they develop, rather than a perfect manager-in-training who can't perform up to snuff when he or she hits the store. Here is some frustrating news for the aggressively impatient: Most *leadagers* become great by steeping in their role over relatively long periods of time. Much like tea dunked in water that becomes stronger with lengthy immersion, your skills will become stronger over time with continued practice, diligence, and feedback you actually synthesize.

Being "underwater" is also a classic business cliché, referring to difficult conditions that leave you gasping for air. At the swimming pool, you can *practice* holding your breath *and build up to* staying under water longer. In hospitality management, the opposite is true. You likely will have to "jump in the deep end," also known as doing the job before you have apprenticed at it. Basically, your primary early focus becomes survival. This of course is a big reason why turnover is so high for many hospitality management positions (not everywhere but enough to call it a "problem"). It is easy to "burn out" when your main function is to keep from drowning.

If you desire to increase your capacity and move quickly up the professional ladder, then immerse yourself in the resources that help define achievement—jump in with hands-on operational practice, read all available company training materials, join peer associations, subscribe to trade publications, and find a mentor who can provide sage advice. You can also eliminate many surprises if you request feedback on your performance prior to annual reviews.

This aggressive, self-directed approach to professional development can bring about the following two distinct outcomes: (1) it will provide a better chance to successfully operate in any hospitality business environment, and (2) it will show that you are trying to prepare yourself and your capacity to adapt and handle anything thrown your way.

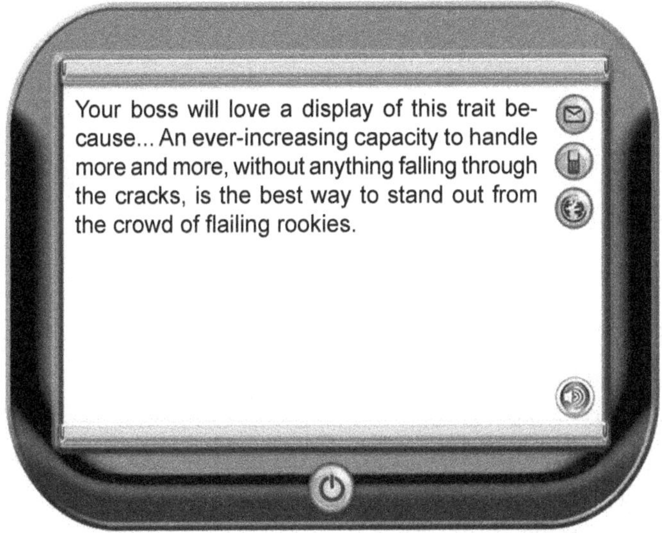

I like the immersion analogy since this is how development and great changes are triggered for many people—boot camp, flight-training simulators, dependency recovery programs, jump school, and so forth. It also aligns with the fact that you "go live" and are playing for keeps every time you open the doors to the public.

With aggressive immersion as opposed to just "getting your feet wet," you can create bigger waves and better results. In fact, this could very well be the reason so many ol' school bosses chose to make managers suffer through a survival-of-the-fittest rite of passage. Without a prioritized development plan (perhaps because of a seemingly inexhaustible supply of personnel), it may at one time have seemed reasonable to throw the new kids off the dock and see which ones were strong enough to keep themselves from drowning. This approach, however, when not agreed to in advance, can lead to wet-cat hissing n' fussing company representatives, coupled with high turnover and other costly problems. If you are not yet practicing any immersion techniques, perhaps you are still passing through somebody's training program.

The best-case scenario of a company training program is that they are providing you with the tools with which you will build the foundation for a fabulous career. The worst-case scenario is that they will treat you like cattle. Aren't you eagerly awaiting your ear tags, vaccinations, and dehorning? *At the risk of repeating the obvious: You are in charge of your own immersion program.*

RIGHTEOUSLY RIGHT DIRECTION

There is a book that is famous in acting circles (are you not on a stage?) titled *An Actor Prepares* by Constantine Stanislavski; it is an interesting read. The main transferrable point for *leadagers* is that everyone who is great at what they do has spent a good deal of time preparing and practicing. (Are you not looking for a "method" to the madness?) Most eager and youthful professionals could benefit from a reminder that commitment and preparation are choices you make that can greatly contribute toward the building of your confidence. Confidence and competence are two of the key building blocks of successful careers, and only the rarest of the rare can succeed without commitment, practice, and preparation.

So sit back in your chair and answer this question: Have you taken the time to assess where you are in the world today and where you would like to be? I'm talking program, priorities, and performance plan, not your current physical location.

Surely you have been asked by teachers, friends, future in-laws, or coworkers what you're all about. *What have you done and what do you hope to accomplish? In what direction are you headed?* Can you easily answer these questions? If you can't, other people will fill in the blanks for you, like it or not, which will lead to confusion and frustration on your part and theirs.

I am not trying to get you to define today the master plan for the rest of your life. Rather, I'm merely suggesting an alignment exercise you should undertake if you have not already done so. You certainly can alter it as you develop stronger viewpoints and gain experience, but for now, start with those things that come easily and that you are willing to put into action. (As a friend of mine once said, "Yo, just layin' some tracks in the righteously right direction.")

Now that you have been tapped to be a *leadager*, this internal work becomes critical. You may find it hard to swallow, but it is reasonable for any employer to expect that you have sorted out what you stand for, not just what you stand against. Most people can prattle on for hours about the things they don't like, but it's important that you can declare a purpose, vision, and identity for your professional life. A collective display of decisiveness, discipline, and drive will also be looked upon as admirable. Once your thoughts, values, and actions are aligned, you have a foundation for strong *leadager* performance. This platform will assist you in creating depth and authenticity, which are necessary for credibility and your *long-term* success.

Your faith, school, parents, or peers have conditioned you and helped to shape your values. As a *leadager*, a broad perspective is helpful to have in your toolbox as a unifying guide for your department, staff, team, or, as I prefer, tribe.

Try the following commonsense values on for size:

- Alive is better than dead.
- Healthy is better than sick.
- Being early is better than being late.
- Freedom is better than incarceration.
- Practical knowledge is better than practically ignorant.
- Justice is better than injustice.
- Good hygiene is better than body odor.
- Civility is better than rudeness.
- Businesses that turn a profit are better than businesses that don't (unless they are nonprofit, and they still have to take in equal to or more than goes out).

And on it goes…

The remarkably simple "better than" comparisons have been the catalysts for cultural shifts, political revolutions, and human progress for a long time. Surely, you might see a personal benefit in adopting these or other values as the things for which you are willing to speak up, stand up, and maybe even strive toward.

FIREWALL OF VALUES

If you don't yet know what you stand for and how to define your values, look inside yourself. Values are things that resonate within the core of your being; they are your deeply held beliefs. Your values should hold fast and true no matter how they are tested. If you have no values, then you have no anchors, nothing to grab on to when times are tough. You are going to be blown this way and that by external forces rather than being directed internally by the propulsion of your choosing. (When you are "underwater" in a business setting, values serve as your rescue beacon in the night.)

Strong values serve as a firewall, protecting you from the incessant viral tempting and off-the-rails beckoning of instant gratification. Firmly placed values reinforce your long-term plan, which is also called the ability to look and work toward the "big picture." The shared values between individuals in a workplace or living space, is called a culture. It doesn't matter who promotes the culture—bottom up or top down. If there is behavior normalizing "this is how we do things here," it is describing a culture. Cultural values can be cancerous (e.g., "We *all* lie, cheat, and steal"), or inspirational (e.g., "We *never* lie, cheat, or steal"), and can hinge on one word or one person. (See? I told you leadership is an important part of management.)

We all know that value statements—or missions—for business enterprises fade in and out like fads. But it is *nice* if the company you hope to work for, or are working for, has taken the time to develop one. You can then use this to align your values against theirs and assess whether or not there is a fit. Practically speaking, we must recognize that many companies have lofty ideals that never really translate into the day-to-day reality for most employees. Not from lack of effort; it's just super difficult to pull off.

However, it is important for *you* to develop your own mission statement, a set of personal goals that can be outlined in a *Vivid Victory Vision (V3)* or *Head/Heart Orientation (H_2O, your chosen purpose)* to help guide your life (see Chapter 6 for *H_2O* details). These frameworks are simply foundations for deciding in advance what is important to you both in business or personally. They guide you through the multitude of decisions and choices every person must face. The time and discipline devoted to predefining your values and goals pales when compared to the time and effort wasted by having to retrofit values or goals into a hasty decision.

If you have defined your values and goals and aligned them with your actions, you will find that when faced with decisions, 92 percent of your choices will be obvious. This decreases your distractions and improves your odds of successfully accomplishing the stated objectives. (Go on, read it again; I'll wait right here.)

I define my *Vivid Victory Vision (V3)* through my *Great Eight!* All my actions are intended to move these goals forward:

1. Healthy mind, body, and spirit (If you are sick, how can you give your all?)
2. Clear alignment of my values and actions (If you are not a person of your word, who are you?)
3. Harmony with my family, faith, and fate (Your job alone does not make a life.)
4. Maximize the gift of time on Earth ('Nuff said!)
5. Expand my mindfulness and usefulness (Use it or lose it!)
6. Increase my prosperity (Wealth is measured by more than money.)
7. Light frequent inner bonfires (Internally generated enthusiasm warms your bones when faced with the chill wind of adversity.)
8. Continually hone my creative endurance (Don't be a dinosaur; adapt to changing conditions.)

TIME MANAGEMENT

There are many tools available to assist you in staying on point. At the top of the list, would be you, adopting a time management system. Time management is an extremely valuable skill for a *leadager* to develop. The aforementioned values exercise, when paired with a modicum of diligence and a touch of rudimentary systemization, will help to hone your time management skills. As you have seen by now, as your responsibilities increase, the time you have to participate in various activities diminishes. If you don't attempt to manage your time by focusing your undertakings, the results will be as haphazard as your approach. (Again, you must decide what the best use of your time is and then spend the bulk of your time doing those things. (Helpful hint: less "hanging out," alcohol, television, gambling, surfing, texting, and so on.)

I realize that some of this content borders on prescriptive philosophy and that many of you have already figured out what works for you. However, my mongrel voice of experience is barking loudly. A sizable chunk of folks whom I have worked with over the years chose to ignore, or table, this developmental stage and have struggled unnecessarily with the larger aspects of their job.

Meeting topics:

- How do you define a clutch performance?
- How do you practice your *leadager* skills?
- How do you build tribal ties in your group?
- How have you immersed yourself professionally?
- What are the cultural values of your workplace? Are they what they need to be?
- Have you a *Great Eight* or *Vivid Victory Vision* equivalent?
- Are you employing a time management system in your professional life?

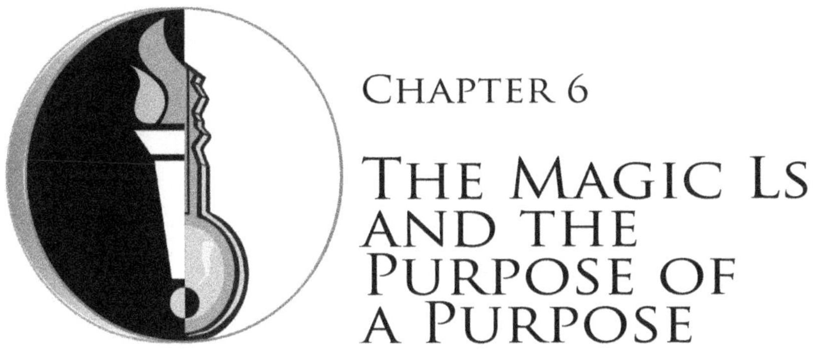

Chapter 6

The Magic Ls and the Purpose of a Purpose

There are vastly different approaches to business and many definitions of success. Similarly, while there exists a plethora of hospitality company mission, vision, and value statements and strategies, it is worth noting that, irrespective of who drafts a set of lofty business ideals, most all of them share a key business goal in common: The company and its senior management want to drive excellence in all respects to the forefront of the guest experience. (Décor, product, service, and quality or system excellence don't just "sorta" happen.) I'm sure you have heard of "walking the walk," not just "talking the talk."

By accepting a managementship position, you will run head-long into a leadership dilemma of universal proportions. It is now "on you" to persuade your team/tribe to do the right thing, at the right time, all or almost all day long. The mere weight of this responsibility (among other pressures and stressors) has affected some people to such a degree that their physical health suffers. Some people break down under this strain. The myth is that the weight of leadership can "bend you." Some "old-timers" may have a slouch in posture, or even become "slow-a-foot," and therefore, are said to be "walkin' heavy."

When you are walkin' heavy, you may be outwardly displaying the strain of your responsibilities and concerns. A heavy walker might be shouldering a heavier burden, but he or she is *also* being offered an abundance of opportunities to exhibit a sense of purpose and display inner strength.

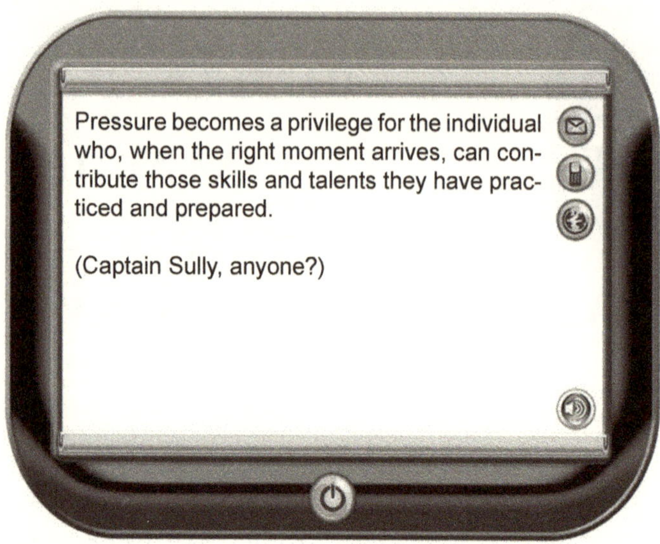

A strong purpose gives you a reason to endure the stress and vagaries of management responsibilities, while at the same time better preparing you to face life in general. To give you a running start, I'm going to divulge my response to the dreaded question (often asked) by interviewers or seminar instructors: "Why are you here?"

Most of us know H_2O is the elemental symbol used for water. Water is a necessity for human life but as long as it is readily available consumption becomes blasé. We need water to live but it is not what most of us live for. Now, if you've been without water for a day or two, the thought of finding water might be all-consuming. If you run dry of a purposeful intent, then you might find yourself attempting all sorts of hijinks, in order to fill your empty well. The pursuit of a valued purpose can consume a lifetime but a life in pursuit lacks the living that accompanies confidently knowing where the next drink is coming from. I use H_2O to frame a context, to serve as a familiar reminder, if you don't carry your own purpose when you are out walking in the world you are gonna get thirsty and if you get thirsty enough, you might quaff any drink offered to you, even if it's a cup of B.S. I bring my own purpose wherever I go, and then I don't desperately guzzle out of someone else's cup. This is my H_2O (*Heart/Head Orientation)* response to the (big) questions I have asked myself. Use this as a start to defining your own foundational cornerstone, or perhaps just to impress the next interviewer. (Drum roll, please!)

The Magic Ls (Magical; get it?)

To labor—To work hard; to exert my energy

To laugh—To live well; to express joy

To learn—To gain knowledge of, or skill in, things; to grow

To lift—To participate in raising things to a higher level

To light—To provide radiant energy by which I, and/or others, can view a path

To love—To exalt truth and beauty; to care

Why these words over all others?

They convey a positive perspective. They represent the limitless promise and capacity that resides in all of us (as proven by the greats). Most assuredly when applied in concert, this collection of traits separates civilization from beasts. In humanity, these are some damn good reasons for living.

The opposite of all of the above would be a negative basis for your actions. I'm sure you have noticed the popular fascination with bad news and sadness that is infused throughout the media, even stalking us through e-mail pop-ups, talking heads on TV and radio, and magazine cover pages.

What you pay attention to, what you think about, what you work on in your personal time is a matter of choice. So why not organize your pursuit around things that will build your positive skill set, not your neutral or negative skills?

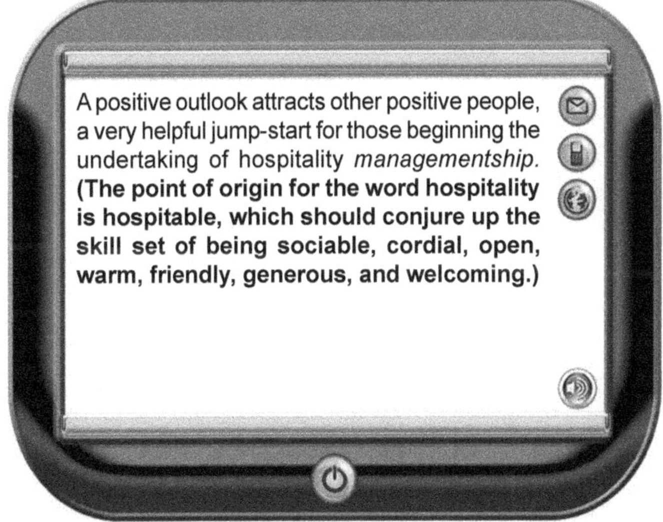

I am not a proponent of the school of thought that says you should automatically expect happiness in life or that you deserve happiness in the workplace. (It's great to have, but there are no guarantees for any of us.) At the same time, it is certainly logical that when your efforts are focused toward a certain outcome, you increase your chances of achieving it. Therefore, by focusing on the above *L* words, you can channel momentum toward constructive, *hopeful* possibilities and away from the deconstructive, *hopeless* plane of view.

In a further effort to reinforce the Magic Ls, I offer the following collection of powerful quotations:

"Great minds have purposes, others have wishes."
—*Washington Irving*

"He who labors diligently need never despair,
for all things are accomplished by diligence and labor."
—*Menander*

"A multitude of small delights constitutes happiness."
—*Charles Baudelaire*

"What is life but the angle of vision? A man is measured by the angle at which he looks at objects. What is life but what a man is thinking all day? This is his fate and his employer. Knowing is the measure of the man. By how much we know, so much we are."
—*Ralph Waldo Emerson*

"Were a star quenched on high,
For ages would its light,
Still traveling downward from the sky,
Shine on our mortal sight.
So when a great man dies,
For years beyond our ken,
The light he leaves behind him lies
Upon the paths of men."
—*Henry Wadsworth Longfellow*

"There is a land of living and a land of dead and the bridge is love, the only survival, the only meaning." —*Thorton Wilder*

(In this case, "dead" has both a figurative and literal meaning, dontcha agree?)

This *choosing* of what you are about is really benchmarking your ascension to adulthood, a willingness to accept responsibility, to commit to a direction, and to prioritize what really matters. You may find that this type of alignment feels unnatural and uncomfortable at first, but the payoff for you and those of us who have to work with you is huge. Stick with it!

Meeting topics:

- What opportunity accompanies "walkin' heavy"?
- Why are you here?
- Define the word "hospitality."
- In nature, something without purpose is called...?

As a *leadager,* this type of life orientation provides an overarching, long-term framework for aligning your actions with purposes that are both personally and professionally useful. Focusing on these areas is continually challenging and surprisingly rewarding in very profound ways.

And finally, ponder this: In the natural world, something without a purpose is called...useless...a dead end...or even—Mr. or Ms. Soon-to-Be Extinct.

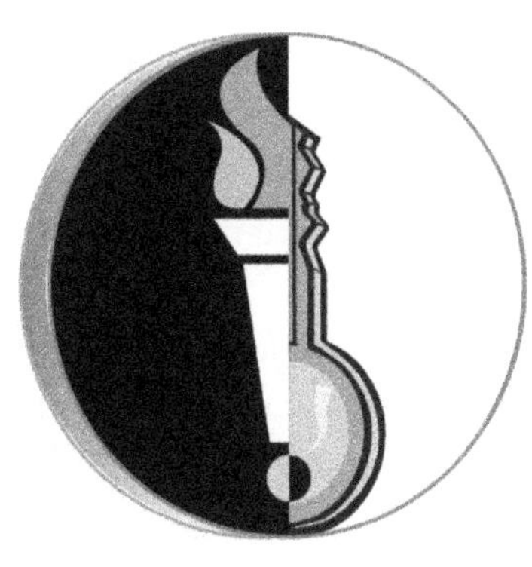

Chapter 7
Duality Maze

After you finish chowin' down on the last chapter's food-for-thought buffet, my goal is to clearly illustrate the necessity for having pre-established authentic values and a defined purpose by way of a little glimpse into your future. Hopefully, your common sense (which is rather uncommon) will lead you toward accepting all the navigational assistance I can provide as you float on the murky waters of your new position.

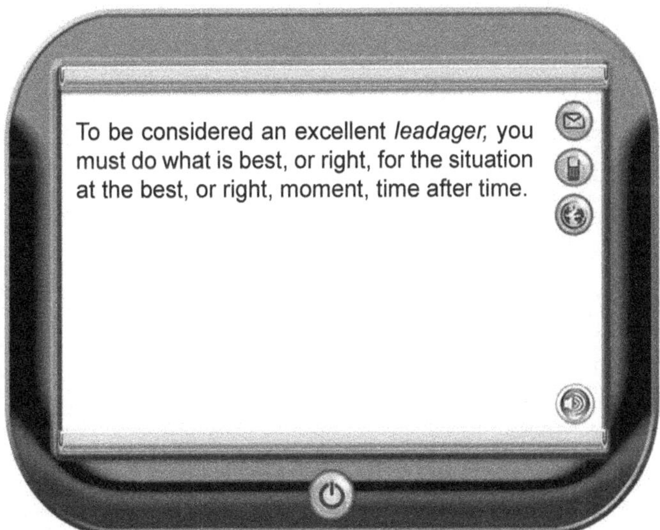

Let's say you have just completed your training and are ready to charge into your first solo day. You will likely be greeted with (1) some inherited staff "confliction," (2) an unresolved cleanliness/maintenance issue, (3) an unforeseen mini crisis, and/or (4) a task/to-do list left unfinished by the last manager on duty. Completing/resolving all of these things will seem virtually impossible once you encounter the harsh reality of *equal but opposite*—conundrums—an unavoidable aspect of the hospitality manager's life.

In the middle of "the rush," somebody needs change for a "C-note"; the toilet is overflowing in the ladies' room; table fifteen wants to talk to a manager; the new busser halts you mid-stride as he slowly mangles his second language, and after what feels like an eternity of confusion, you decipher that he has discovered "funny smoke" inside the walk-in cooler; a server who has just been dumped via a text message is raisin' a ruckus in the kitchen; and two phone calls are on hold for you—one is your significant other and the other is your boss. Okay, have at it.

When the spit hits the fan, do you really think you will properly prioritize your efforts if you don't have a solid foundation that can keep you calm and clear-headed as you chop a path out of the chaos?

If all the above has your head spinning, let's slow things down for a moment. I once worked for two crusty guys who were partners in a number of hospitality operations. They were a couple of ego-centric, ego-driven, *eee-go-away* bosses. Early one evening, during the dawn of my career, I was running the floor shift when one of these sweethearts came by to check up on things. He pulled me aside and declared that the background music was "too damn loud." I scurried off to remedy this transgression, running smack into owner number two, who had arrived through another doorway. He hailed me over to say he was going next door but wanted me to turn up the music as it was "too damn soft." (They did this kind of thing all the time.) There it was in a nutshell...a conundrum. I was facing a paradox, or perhaps even a direct conflict. Who should I please? What is the right thing to do? How do I quickly travel through the maze? My solution on that day was to pretend to scurry off to do their bidding, then report back to both that the problem was solved after deciding the volume level was fine. I wasn't trying to be a jerk, but I did get tired of them jerking me around. They thought it was funny to countermand each other's orders, and the staff and the guests suffered because of their lack of professionalism.

You will be given repetitive tasks that will evolve into tangible, marketable skills—inventory, cash reconciliation, scheduling, cooking, and so on. However, also inherent in your new role will be the insidious, "Do both, or all, of these things, now" aspect that you will find continuously befuddling.

It will be helpful if you read the following quote a couple times:

"The test of a first rate intelligence is the ability to hold two opposed ideas in the mind at the same time, and still retain the ability to function. One should, for example, be able to see things that are hopeless and yet be determined to make them otherwise."—F. Scott Fitzgerald

Routinely (every day) your big challenge will be figuring out how to accomplish the following things (and dozens of others with a similar nature) at the same time:

- To administrate and participate
- To welcome diversity and drive unity
- To be responsive to the present and responsible to the future
- To forge strong relationships and keep a suitable distance
- To think outside, and act within, the boundaries
- To be patient with people's personalities and aggressive with people's performance
- To maintain direction and allow for disagreement
- To over-communicate and keep your mouth shut
- To be quick (but not impulsive) and thoughtful (but not slow)
- To have coexisting doubt and faith
- To grow the top and bottom lines

Business Coordination

So how do you achieve the accomplishment of both when, at times, they seem to be in direct conflict? Based on my observations, regular Joe/Jill managers minimize this type of challenge by prioritizing one *over* the other because of bias, inexperience, or a just-forget-it avoidance attitude. Yet if your goal is to excel, you will view these conflicting conundrums as *leadager* training ground zero. The more of these situations to which you are subjected, the better off you are. This is also referred to as paying your dues, earning your stripes, or collecting rookie cookies.

The only real way out of this is by going through it. The often overlooked fact (by the uninitiated) is that on any job, you will have to create a "trading currency." You will be tested to see what you can handle (by the principal player's reckoning, not yours). This is also known as developing "street cred." In the *WOW*, nobody will truly trust or willingly follow *you* until *you* prove that *you* know what you are talking about.

The developmental benchmarks (or acumen) you should focus on during this period are the equivalent of possessing a strong right and left arm, a quick left and right brain, and effective soft and hard skills. The more you utilize *all* of your resources, the easier it will be to respond to the inevitable forthcoming yins and yangs. Think of it this way: You are in hot pursuit of *business coordination*, a graceful exhibition of balance in motion. (It is best to think of yourself as always in motion.) Constantly do all you can to identify and strengthen your weaker *leadager/managementship* skills (a sorta endless and slightly daunting commitment, no?).

Talent and desire in and of themselves are not enough to achieve greatness. To truly become a great *leadager*, you have to leverage all of your hard-won experiences into a solid, results-filled record over an extended period of years. If this sounds difficult, take heart, nobody gets it right all the time. In reality, you only have to be right a *majority* of the time and usually it is only the bigger things that count. (Helpful hint: Getting the *most* out of *most things* is a more realistic goal than getting "all there is to get" out of any *one* thing.) Shooting for absolute perfection at any one part of your job becomes the enemy of doing

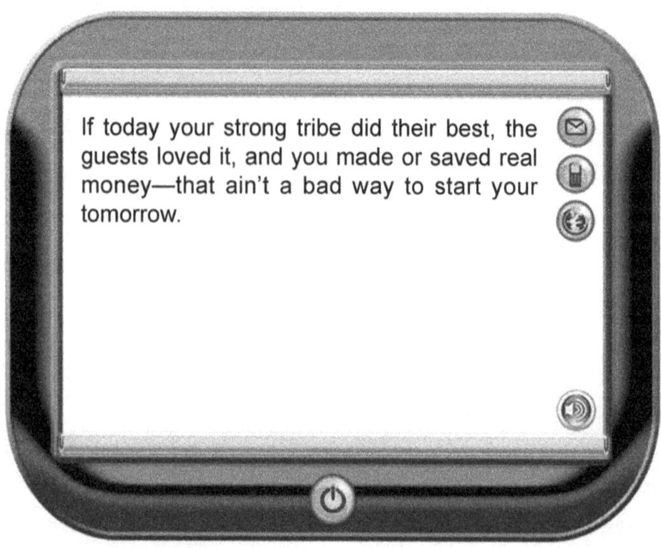

a perfectly acceptable or above average job in all areas. There is not enough time or resources to achieve perfection twenty-four/seven in the hospitality business. There are too many parts moving way too fast.

VOICES AND CHOICES

Many of the boldest and most successful *leadagers* don't have complete, let alone perfect, information when faced with making a decision. True *leadagers* surround themselves with smart people they can trust and can poll for facts and perspectives. Still, they often end up going with a hopeful leap of faith or gut instinct when making decisions. It behooves you to learn the difference between collecting *comprehensive* information and collecting *crucial* information before sealing any decision.

Comprehensive information is the collection of all that is known and accessible. *Crucial* information is limited to what is important for making *this* decision.

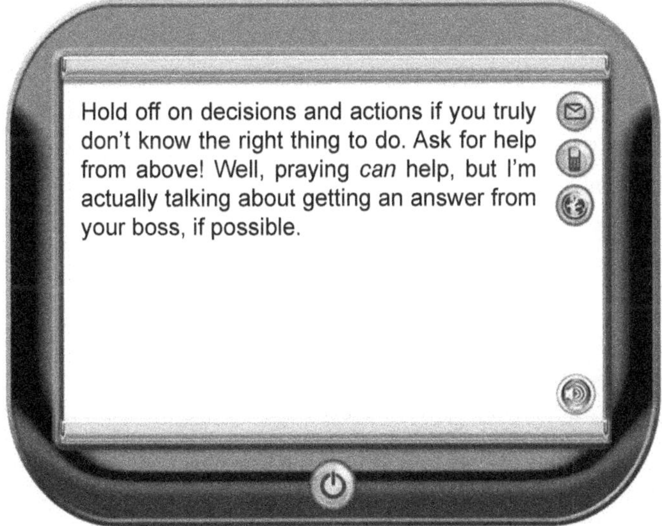

Most business decisions are made under the pressure of severe time constraints, and it is not always possible to draw directly from previous experiences. Brand-new "stuff" will be thrown at you all the time. Oh, and if this were not enough, there is the dicey matter of the accuracy and credibility of the information on which you are basing your decisions (i.e., things you think you know that might not be true; things you want to know that can't be found, and so on). So always operate as if you don't "know it all." When you act as if you do know it all, it may prevent people from bringing you any new news—and this is a place to take caution. You want always to encourage your tribe to bring you information, so take care not to overtly discourage—or mess up—this early warning system, as it may be your key to heading off problems before they become disasters. Do take heart, however, for with added "seasoning" (a word so dreaded by the uninitiated), typical hospitality business scenarios do become familiar and solutions do become semi-apparent.

All of this illuminates the need for an operational tracking system that provides "real time" metrics and statistics you can use as a shorthand guide for directional decisions.

INSIDE SCOOP

And now...I will shed some light on a—not so little—secret of organizational life. There are some overeager beavers who deftly scramble up the political and positional ladder seemingly salivating at the prospect of power. Their mastery of corporate gamesman/woman-ship does not guarantee that they are the "sharpest knives in the drawer." All too often, my experience has shown that if you were to strip away their job title, many lack the influence or substance for making critical decisions.

Ironically, at times it is the awkward foot-draggers who are more capable of making good decisions but are unwilling to be pressured into making them and don't want to be held accountable. This leads me to an important point: Lots of smart and entirely good people have discovered they don't have what it takes to manage things or lead others.

Leadagers who possess good business judgment, a strong sense of direction, and a willingness to accept the conditions of urgency and accountability without a seedy, overcoat-flashing of their fundamental character flaws are the ideal package. Companies spend a lot of money trying to nurture or "home grow" these traits. Unfortunately, this can be an elusive combination of qualities. Conversely, a lack of motivation, butt-headedness, and proven idiocy lead to professional euthanasia every time. (Trust me on this; the latter traits are pretty darn common.)

So let's face it. You will have to make many decisions without the experience or the information you may desperately think you need, and inevitably, you will decide incorrectly. *You will be wrong,* and hopefully, someone will allow you to learn from your mistakes. It might be timing, support from the powers that be, or just luck that saves your job.

Early in your career, one of the most important things to learn is *how to be wrong in the right way.*

Being wrong the right way looks like this:

- You made what you thought were sound decisions, striving not to be irresponsible, ignorant, or prejudicial.
- You can explain your thought process with respect to how you came to the decision in a logical manner.
- Your values were aligned with the organization's values.
- You have shown good judgment on previous occasions.
- You display a willingness to learn from your mistakes.

If you did all the above, you should come out okay (assuming you didn't burn the place to the ground).

All new *leadagers* should be allowed some time to practice alternating the gas, clutch, and brake pedals of *managementship* (i.e., multitasking and managing/weighing multiple—and sometimes conflicting—priorities, such as chewing gum and running with scissors for all of you nondriving types). The fact is most managers are playing the standard game of "catch up" in a starkly maniacal fashion. I strongly urge you to grow away from being the *hapless prey-of-the-day*—as events pounce on you—and strive to get ahead of events by becoming a *predator of pro-activity*, turning activities into accomplishments and churning problems into opportunities.

It could be that you are now launching toward this orbit of professional pro-activity because: (1) you have a superb mentor, (2) you joined an organization devoted to professional growth of all its members, and (3) you have experienced enough "seasoning" events that your sixth sense is now kicking in and you are able to smell the smoke before you see the fire.

Employing a combination of all of the aforementioned circumstances is the ideal medley for companies to use in developing *leadagers* who are in the ramp-up phase of their careers. But be warned that this is the exception rather than the rule. Most companies are unable or unwilling to fund a steady stream of bad decisions, nor are they staffed with senior leadership who truly will commit to your professional development as part of their personal objectives. Enlightened senior *leadagers*, however, know that the road to becoming great is a process. Mistakes, even those deemed failures, provide a developmental experience that can be a *profound* opportunity for both individual and organizational growth.

Many Joe and Jill guard dog managers still tend to rely on a fear-based approach to move the dial. Typically, it also includes barking threats, public admonishments, indiscriminate venting, "blame gaming," and a fair amount of CYA. This stereotypical low-level management profile is the bane of our industry and in my experience it exists almost everywhere. I'm not saying people and events in business won't conspire to make for some pretty tough days, but opening the gates to the local sewage treatment plant and dumping the contents downhill will not be viewed as practicing the highest level of leadership.

I guess the existence of these guard dog managers could be a direct offshoot of hospitality management having a "low barrier of entry." (No advanced degree or standardized professional apprenticeships are required for the front of the house, with the possible exception of some very fine dining establishments or traditionally run hotels.) It might also be that some people just don't want to work on themselves, believing instead that correcting others is the best use of their time.

BUFFOONVILLE

So when trying to grow into new responsibility levels how does one avoid the early hits that can be so demoralizing? Do everything possible to avoid working for buffoons, particularly in companies that show themselves to value and promote buffoons into positions of authority and power. Run away from these companies. Ultimately, only charismatic, attractive, politically savvy buffoons rise to the top of the buffoon pile in these organizations—the empty-suit buffoons who are a mile wide and an inch deep. And once you have a Grand PooBah Buffoon who is now running Buffoonville, it's just one big crap-fest from an integrity, morale, and cultural perspective. Oh—and then they file for Chapter 11.

Listen up: This summation has been expertly provided by my wife who happens to be in the business of finding top executives for multibillion-dollar businesses. Despite the monkey-business tonality of her lingo, her advice is right on and should not be taken lightly

(Hmm...I might have caught her on a bad day). Organizations reflect the personalities and values of the most powerful people within their walls. In general, this is the way of the world. Think back to high school—geeks, gangbangers, cheerleaders, jocks, gearheads, and stoners—and don't you agree, a fair-sized bunch of buffoons? That bunch of buffoons all go out and get jobs and/or start companies. The chances are great that you will run into them, somewhere, at some point in your career.

There is, however, an alternative to Buffoonville. Have you ever heard of compound interest? This process allows you to make a steady contribution to your savings plan and over a long period of time, thanks to accruing interest, grow your nest egg into a big basket of eggs. Well, I have a different slant on this. I suggest that there exists such a thing as *compound work experience.*

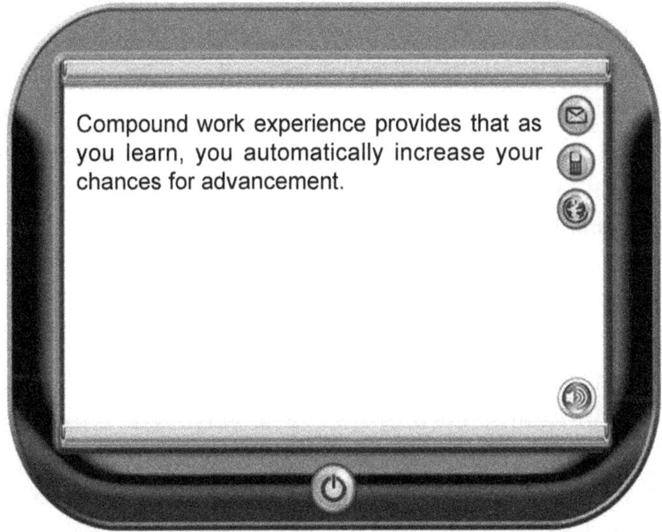

Compound work experience is acquired by (1) working for the best *leadager* organizations, (2) working for a *leadager*-mentor, (3) working where the opportunities for advancement are plentiful, and (4) working where the varieties of experience are bountiful. This is a workplace where you are allowed to challenge yourself and to grow; a place where accepting more responsibility will eventually translate into more money for you; a place that acknowledges/nurtures your involvement/participation and consistently shows appreciation for your contributions; a place that holds you accountable when you don't contribute; and ultimately, a place that provides value to you through means that are not purely financial.

It is worth noting that I am not focusing on how many hours you might have to work, what benefits are included, what uniform you'll wear, where you live, or what kind of vibe the place gives you. Although they may or may not be important to you, these items are not integral to compound work experience. Again, this sort of contemplation should make it apparent to you why you must, at the outset of your career, begin with the values and accompanying tradeoff assessment before you begin your climb to managementship so you know precisely what is important to you.

We all know life is reasonably viewed as a series of tradeoffs. I can have this or that, but probably not both. I can accept a good-paying job in another state, but I won't be in close proximity to my family. I could lick door knobs, but I would then have to accept the ensuing assault on my immune system from the germs in residence and so on.

I had a friend who dreamed of owning a house, but not just any house. He wished for a home with a yard with a swimming pool and large enough to accommodate his kids and dogs. He was hardworking, but not wealthy, and it took him quite a while to realize his goal. When he finally moved into the house of his dreams (after a lot of sweat equity on his part), he was very happy and proud. He celebrated with a housewarming party and invited a few friends and relatives over.

Things were off to a grand start. He was basking in compliments over his work and the guests were having a swell time. Then his father-in-law, after downing a few brewskies, gruffly barked, "How in the holy hell can you stand all these planes?" You see, the only way my friend could afford this dream was to buy a home close to the airport. As enveloped as he was in the positive aspects of what he had achieved, he chose to disregard/devalue the flight-path noise factor. His father-in-law, on the other hand, could not get over the jet noise, which was at the top of his "home buying mistakes" list.

Irrefutably, your values and your tradeoff tolerance are inextricably linked. You must clarify your assessments. What do you value? What will you sacrifice to achieve your *Victory Vision?* Answering these questions will require an *ongoing and thorough participation on your part.*

WEIGHTED VALUES ARE THE KEY

Meeting topics:

- How do you navigate through the daily duality maze?
- How does a person build "trading currency" in the workplace?
- Why is "getting the most, out of the most" a realistic goal?
- What are your best business metrics?
- How can you be wrong in the right way?
- What are weighted values?

When facing an important decision, many advice-dispensers suggest taking a sheet of paper, drawing a line down the middle, and writing at the top of each side *pros* and *cons*—as in, what's good and bad about whatever you are facing. Do *not* use this approach without assigning *weighted values* to the details. What's the most important stuff? For each individual, all the ingredients that go into the process of decision-making do not carry the same value or weight. Some items may clearly be more important to you or your family than they might be to someone else. This is why it is so important to have already spent some time ruminating on your values before you step into the big leagues of *managementship* where choices and decisions affect more than just yourself.

In order to find an opportunity that allows for *compound work experience,* you must search, assess, and evaluate the tradeoffs. This, by the way, is vastly different than conveniently going to the nearest buffoon factory and applying for a job…any job. Take a shot at the job that gets you in the door of the right place with the right people for where you want to go. If you don't know where you want to go, or where you want to be, for gosh sakes, start by figuring that out.

Chapter 8

Mundane Rain Motivation

Have you thought about the daily investment you can make in yourself while also serving others as a *leadager?* Perhaps you believe your current job is not worthy of your best effort, or maybe you've become disheartened or disillusioned. Have you had your fill of being judged, analyzed, or inspected? Set all that aside. What you must "buy into" is the fact that *you* are worthy of your best effort. So in addition to paying the bills, this job is also providing you with a place to practice (practice is important and will pay off big) this stuff and get paid for it. If you maximize your effort investment in this two-for-one growth opportunity, you will create a better future for you and your organization. Perhaps, more to the point, you will be preparing yourself to meet life's challenges so you may more fully take advantage of future opportunities that come your way.

Do you truly comprehend the awesome array of opportunities that exist throughout your workday allowing you to practice significant life skills? Many management jobs require a lot of repetition: count this, schedule that, open/close, open/close, double-check, triple-check. Rote routines can produce "day-walking," the notable and notorious illness of sleepwalking through a shift. But the beauty of *management-ship* is that your time spent on the job also provides the opportunity to practice positive habits and skills that easily transfer to your life outside of work.

Wake up and consider the following: Do you believe your ability to focus, be responsible, generate enthusiasm, create ideas, follow through on tasks, stick to a budget, forge strong relationships, overcome adversity, and attack goals will ever be a benefit to you outside of work? Dagnabit, the answer is a resounding *yes!*

Realizing the opportunity to integrate your professional development with personal growth becomes a great source of *motivation* on the days when you must drive through *a rain of the mundane.*

Being involved in the *managementship* of any business can be complicated and difficult. Businesses usually require some type of involvement with people. (Uh-oh, problems from the get-go!) They are chock-full of the human condition—fallacies, frustration, missteps, pressure, poor timing, and relentless competition. I would like to suggest the following three *favors* that you can do for yourself to bring about some relief—and motivation.

1. Find a main vein. Work is hard; business is hard; *managementship* is hard; competition is hard. And criticism of your performance is *hard to take.* Many advice dispensers suggest you must discover what you are passionate about (or even love) and then turn that into your career. They suggest this advice simply because if you enjoy most everything about what you are doing, it doesn't feel like work. *That doesn't make it less difficult, just more palatable.* And if you are not in love with what you do, some people will choose one of three paths.

Get the frack out of Dodge and find another job ASAP.

Become a *selfish paycheck zombie*, retired on the job, putting forth minimum care and effort; or even better, a *selfish whip-cracking zombie bastard* who takes out their misery on the backs of others. (Note: This is not to be considered a viable option.)

Or you can identify the people or parts of your job that do, in fact, energize and excite you and draw enthusiasm from that vein as you slog through the distasteful, disappointing, or disastrous rest of the slush. ("I like the money/benefits, but not the work. I like the people, but it's not much money. I like being creative but this pressure is stressful. The job is a dream, but the commute is horrible.")

This is the tradeoff approach most people use while trying to make a living. (This is also called *compromising,* which you might *upliftingly* think of as focusing on the part of a promise with which you have something in common.)

2. Become a connoisseur of systems. I intend for you to draw on the deepest meaning of the word "connoisseur." Try to develop a nose for what a good system looks and acts like. (You should be able to do this without swirling, smelling, swishing, savoring, or spitting.)

In every business there are issues that defy predictability. Bringing order and control to unpredictable elements is a highly desired skill and certain competitive advantage. (Hence, the early invention of a counting system or accounting, as we call it today.)

SYSTEMIZER

Everyone who is involved in running a business wants to project confidently where they will be financially at the end of the year, preferably before the year even starts (a little bit of fortune-telling called forecasting). As a result, there are systems being used for hiring and paying employees, tracking sales, counting cash and generating financial reports, insurance expenses, and maintenance issues. In short, there has been an attempt to systemize everything in business (to ensure the forecasted outcome "comes out").

It is in your best interest to become familiar and comfortable with systems, *especially those your company utilizes.* (How does this work? Why choose this one over that one? And most important, what do we really need our systems to do?) At some point, you personally will be asked to undertake improving the performance of a department, store, or region, and you will maximize your success potential if you can hone or muscle key systems to help you to produce better results. Business systems are the gears that are engaged to realize business results; but like all systems they are dependent on the information, goals, values, and vision that set them in motion (dumb in, dumb out).

If you are limited in your ability to use and leverage the best systems available, you will underachieve by a factor of ten. System success is the recent force that begat the "best practice" approach to business performance improvement (go on, look it up). Strong and proven systems, for example, make it easier to raise money for a franchise business. Road-tested and debugged systems that are not dependent on individuals to work effectively are more bankable. Please remember, however, as you are canoodling with systemization: Systems are not substitutes for successful products, great locations, outstanding service, or spot-on market timing, nor will they make up much ground on bad hires. But don't "pass go" without committing to becoming a systems connoisseur.

3. Learn to speak the royal language. In business, cash is queen (or king, if you prefer). Gotta make it, gotta use it, gotta get more, and gotta keep what you got. It took me a long time to realize that there is an imperial collective of people who use "money know-how" (financial fitness acumen) as their entrée into the *WOW*'s top jobs. And you are nothing to them unless you "know da know." (Come on, now; "liquidity" is a word you use everyday, no?)

There is no way you can be considered for, let alone achieve, a top dream job without walkin' and talkin' dollars and cents. You may be an expert in your area or industry, but to grow or perhaps at times to survive, you may need to travel beyond your personal network to obtain money. It doesn't matter if it is the bank, the boss, or Wall Street; they won't speak the language of your passion, expertise, or dreams. They *will,* however, require you to display your business and financial acumen (on paper, as spoken in percentages of minimized risk and maximized rewards).

Most people who have more money than you will talk money better than you. Here is the short version of almost any money conversation: "Why should I/we give you money instead of doing other things with it?" Buy into this premise; you will have to *compete* numerically to justify/prove your viewpoint. Potential investors will analyze and compare your projected results to more fruitful ways of investing their money (also known as projected return on investment *[ROI]).* This is why you must track all that comes in and all that goes out, not just to pay the bills and buy some fish, but to compete at every level. *(Now you see, Grasshopper, how the score is kept in the real game of business.)* Percentages and comparatives do not require high-level trigonometry, just attention to detail, total commitment, and an understanding of why they matter.

When you begin to hear the following questions, you'll know that your knowledge of the royal language is being tested:

- What are the sales per square foot of your store?
- What are today's sales per labor hour or productivity?
- What is your annual staff turnover ratio running?
- What is the current net profit margin on these sales?
- What are your actual sales compared to budget?
- What is your year to year "comp" sales percentage?

Rather than running away scared or getting embarrassed, you might simply respond, "I do not currently have that information at hand, but I will get back to you later today with those answers." Or the "fall on your sword" confessional response: "Where might I find that information for you?"

Do *not* become a person who shows him- or herself to have little interest in the royal language ("...I dunno"). If you do, it will only be a matter of time before you are labeled as one of the lost souls who don't "get it." If you want to get ahead of the curve, you can prepare yourself by delving into the industry "numbers story." Start with specifics such as the "ideal" food/beverage/labor costs, gross, net, and so forth, then grab the chart of accounts for your store (the snail-trail of all the money out) and read and reread it until following along becomes second nature.

After that, break down the store's monthly profit and loss statement *(P&L)* and get to know it backward and forward. Work your way around an annual budget until it makes sense. Ask questions of anyone who can help deliver this knowledge to you. Ultimately, you should be able to answer for yourself all the questions that might arise from an annual corporate report. A slightly disturbing (as if you have the free time) but practical pursuit is to read business plans for industry concepts and identify the financial risk and reward ratios while looking for any fatal flaws.

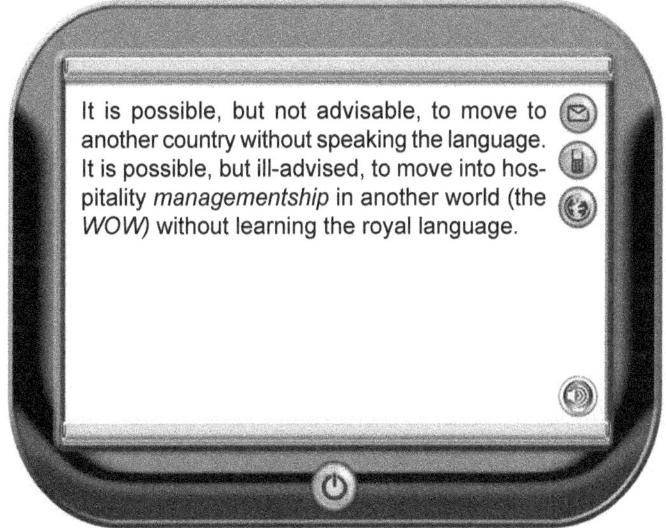

Money is usually the supreme motivator by which employers can entice employees; however, there are simply not enough "topflight jobs" suited for everyone on the planet. If you find yourself lacking the right kind of external motivation, then it is time to muster some internal motivation. And if you still cannot find motivation of any kind, then it may be time to get some coaching from a mental health professional.

Meeting topics:

- What is your professional "main vein"?
- In which business systems do you have expertise?
- Can you speak the royal language in your sleep? Are you teaching it to others?
- How do you engage and motivate others? (Helpful hint: by example, first and foremost.)

Chapter 9
Up in Smoke!

When you are handed the keys to a hospitality kingdom (or queendom), we can assume you have received some level of training to enable you to handle a typical "day in the life." Yet despite preparation and training, things can—and will—go awry on your first solo day. Most of your training and shadowing will not address cataclysmic events. As with everything, preparation for the prevention of worst-case scenarios can help to avoid a multitude of headaches down the line.

Think of it this way: There are metaphorical sets of bear traps just waiting for you all along your new *leadager* pathway. I personally have tromped on many of them as I wandered through my mentor-less early years. I wish for you to avoid as many of these painful lessons as possible.

Early in my career I never gave a second thought to the following items, but in later years it seemed as if these things haunted me. I strongly suggest you process and store this information at the forefront of your managerial mind. (Remember, it is awfully tough to spin a plate that's gone up in smoke.)

- **Food-borne illness.** Once upon a time, there was a prep cook who changed his baby's diaper at home just prior to his shift. He was running late, forgot to wash his hands, and as soon as he got to work, he jumped right into prepping lettuce for salads. That one unsanitary act (1) made about twenty people sick, (2) led the local TV newscast after the Super Bowl, (3) cut store sales in half by the next day, and (4) left the survival of the business touch and go for about eighteen months.

Boom, just like that! In this business you must become a food safety fanatic. Helpful hint: Retrieve the most recent health inspection for your restaurant and *confirm for yourself* that all of the latest issues have been (or will be) corrected. It is much easier and more prudent to do this first thing, rather than later standing in front of a health inspector mumbling weak answers while receiving a citation or fine.

- **Liquor license suspension or revocation.** If the establishment is allowed to serve alcohol, it needs those sales to stay in business. May "all things almighty" help ya if something bad happens to the liquor license during your shift. It is legally impossible to serve booze without a license, and there are always forces looking to take away your licensed beverage service (e.g., stings conducted by the police, community activists, avenging attorneys, servers doing favors for underage friends). You must set a serious tone among all employees with regard to checking IDs and eradicating over-service, even to the extent of paying for a taxi if a guest presents him- or herself as questionable in his or her ability to arrive home safely. Service of licensed beverages is a privilege *and* a heavy responsibility. You must not treat it lightly, and do not allow others to do so. One misstep can put you, or the store, permanently out of business.
- **Robbery with injury.** Many people have lost their lives on the job because they worked for a business deemed to be an easy target by criminals. Think of all the things you can do to deter a criminal act, such as brilliant parking lot lights, strict back door entry procedures, frequent lock changes, daily bank deposits, only opening the safe when the office door is closed, secure smoke break areas (if any exist), video surveillance, and consistent diligence. No amount of money is worth someone getting hurt. You will never overcome the guilt or grief of being in charge when a careless act allows any harm to come to the people who depend on your leadership. Help the tribe to work smart, keep your eyes open, and if it comes down to it, give the criminals all the money. It's a cheap price to pay in order for you to see your families again.
- **Accidents.** Too common are the stories of falls, cuts, and burns, all a function of the number of "parts in motion and

the pace of the place." If a guest or tribe member is ever at risk of injury, you must fix or repair the problem immediately. A negligence lawsuit (translation: you lose big money) originates from a problem that you knew about, or even *should* have known about, but chose to ignore or deny. Push for nonslip footwear and heavy-lifting back supports, and keep knives sharp. From a business culture perspective, constantly build, reinforce, and reward a safe, accident-free mind-set. Dangerous sophomoric behavior should never happen on your watch—whipped cream, soda gun, and ketchup squirt-wars are bad things. Tightening table and chair legs, keeping the floor dry around the ice machine, and ensuring that the blade guard on the slicer is properly installed are all good things. (As a wealthy attorney once said, "It is always easier and cheaper to fix it now than to have to buy your way out once you're in trouble.")

- **Harassment.** Any demeaning, discriminatory workplace behavior becomes a clear indicator of the character, values, goals, and intelligence of the *leadager* and will eventually bleed the organization dry. Sure, there have been an honest few at the top who did not know an employee was being harassed because of his or her sexual orientation, religion, mental/physical challenges, age, and so forth. Although it is challenging to set new standards of ethical behavior, it always begins with the *leadagers* (you are now one of them) setting the example. The tribe culture should be *all for one and one for all* with diversity viewed as an immense plus and an opportunity for new knowledge rather than a wall between us and them. Does this sound like politically correct fluff to you? If so, you have some work to do; your corruption of power could cost the company hundreds of thousands of dollars. By the way, keep your physical contact with coworkers limited to high-fives, handshakes, and fist bumps—never, ever a kiss, grope, or touch in a lingering manner. (FYI: If ever there was a blacklist in our business, it includes managers who are the cause of big legal entanglements.)

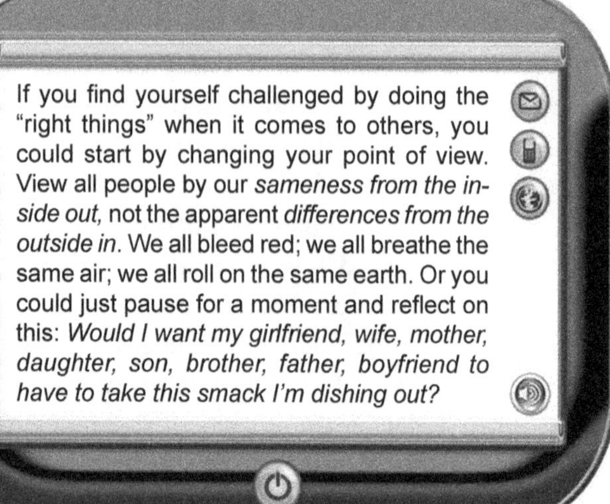

Meeting topics:

- Name your top ten "bad things" that can happen to a hospitality operation.
- What is your group doing to ensure that they don't?

Chapter 10

Take Ten/ Coffee Break

I just threw a lot of heavy stuff your way and we are about to drive over the rocky road that a general manager (*GM)* travels. So I'm going to let you catch your breath and while you're doing that, I'll take a moment to review some of the choice cuts from the first part of this book. You know—pause and reflect on cause and effect.

At some point early on in your career, you will be pulled aside by someone and told that as an "assistant manager" your job is, in simple terms, to execute a good shift. You should expect this, but don't agree to settle for just today's stuff. Whoever tells you this is probably not looking as far down the road as you should be. Of course, they wish that you will go above and beyond whatever reasonable request they have made today. That's called working for a living. Yet you should be unwavering in your dedication toward improving skills that you can use down the road and your dreams of bigger-buck tomorrows.

Great managementship does demand an affinity for practical knowledge, unending personal growth, and a little luck. Now let's summarize a few takeaways from the first nine chapters:

- Early on, you must model the "shift up" requirement that has taken place in your life (i.e., transitioning from just showing up to work as an hourly staffer to leading and really executing [being/doing] the work as a salaried professional).
- Early on, you must start preparing yourself to play a larger role.
- Early on, you must build a purposeful, resilient experience base upon which you can add the pressure of additional work without breaking apart.

- Early on, you must identify the differences between bad, good, and great results, then aggressively move your area of responsibility forward and upward.
- Early on, you must meet head on the challenging circumstances that will present themselves.
- Early on, you must learn to leverage whatever resources you have into wins.

Meeting topics:

- What kind of a foundation are you building for the rest of your career to be based upon?
- How do you define a great shift, month, or year? Is everybody working from that same definition?
- What habits do you utilize to stay healthy?
- Do you like, really like, a challenge?
- Have you learned how to gather your resources and maximize your leverage?

We have spent a lot of time on the concept of *leadagers* and the advantage of practicing plate-spinning. I discussed the purpose of values and the value of having a purpose. We defined wisdom and internal motivation. I even suggested you bring your own H_2O to work.

In athletics, all of the aforementioned would be considered core muscles; a chef might call it a roux; an arborist would call them roots. You will increase your chances of becoming a great *leadager* and an accomplished spinner of plates (who is "pulling in large paper") when, just as in architecture, you build a rock solid foundation to support the rest of your career.

Chapter 11

She'z All Mine Now!

If you have been anointed to the title of general manager (*GM*), then you have persevered through many vicissitudes (your new favorite word), achieved a nod of recognition for your effort, and perhaps, even a long-awaited bump up in salary. You may have been the first choice, the last choice, or the only choice, but there you stand. And look at you now—all this and new shoes with orthopedic supports, too. As the prickly heat of growing responsibility envelops you, be warned: You are now personally accountable *for the actions taken by others that are seemingly beyond your control.*

In addition to your newly acquired skills, you are likely bleary-eyed from your steep learning curve relative to your experiences with equipment, people, paperwork, systems—you name it. So turn your aching head this way and pay a moment of attention to this relevant refresher.

- People don't always act the way they should.
- Many people you work for will not be concerned with the means, only with the desired result. ("Don't tell me about the labor pains; just show me the baby.")
- Conflict depends on the participation level of both parties.
- Mind reading is an imaginary game. (So don't ask for it from others and certainly do not attempt it yourself.)
- Something you value may be treated like dirt by other people.

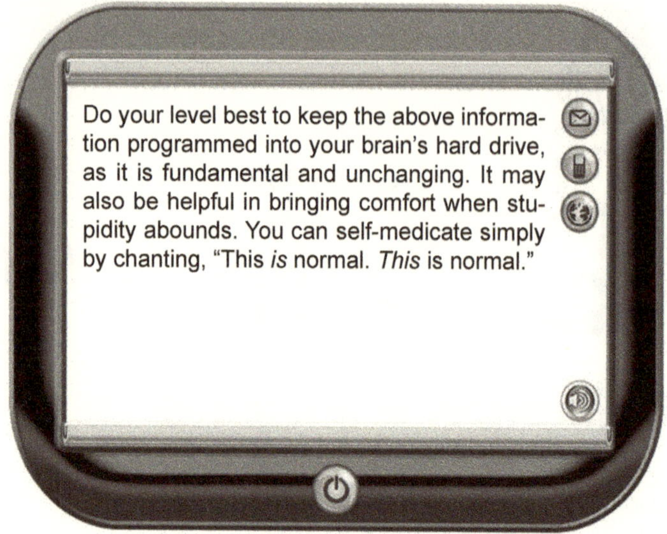

All of these items are amply displayed in the following story handed down to me by my Southern grandpappy.

An ornery, old married couple lived down the road. They owned a ramshackle, tarp-roofed rib shack. Those two seemed to fight about everything, but they hardly owned much of anything. In their later years, they had moved beyond bickering into a full-fledged feud of silence.

When the wife took ill, the cuss of a husband didn't really say much and friends couldn't tell if he was mad, sad, or indifferent about his wife's condition. Her health worsened and he grew more sullen. When she passed away, he remained silent.

As the mourners returned from the gravesite and gathered at the couple's place of business, they began to follow the grieving husband to the front door. When he crested the doorway of the not-fit-for-a-dog shack, those standing closest heard him utter his first words in a month of Sundays. He hissed, "She'z all mine naw," followed by a very wicked cackle.

My friend, it's all *yours* now. (Be careful what you wish for!)

Here is a glimpse at some of my past experiences, some of which may resemble things you are about to encounter. Expect to be spending a lot of your time on unexpected occurrences.

- I have lost count of the number of restroom trashcan fires I have extinguished. (Is there an arsonist club that gives points for this activity?)

- I uncovered unbelievable embezzlement schemes that were used by many formerly trusted tribe members on every job I have ever held.
- I busted one of my managers who had a side hobby of taking pictures of young women with their shirts pulled up in exchange for drinks. (After not-so-careful consideration, he had selected the local sheriff's daughter for participation, thus quickly ending his predilection and career.)
- As a *GM,* I have been offered thimblefuls and fistfuls of illegal drugs, all in an attempt to convince me to let underage patrons enter the premises or consume alcoholic beverages. (At least 50 percent were likely sting set-ups, but *which* 50 is, of course, the second best reason not to go there.)
- I was promoted after I told the truth about my supervisor's on-the-clock overindulgence with the ("it's not really drinking if you drink...") sweet Chablis, becoming the youngest *GM* in the history of the company. I was hung out to dry when, after two weeks, they rehired said manager to be my assistant manager. Turned out he was the owner's brother-in-law and two weeks was more than enough to dry out, right? (Maybe I should have found that out *before* I turned the light on in that particular cockroach-filled room.)
- I was turned into a sacrificial lamb for a state liquor board after hiring an employee who was using fake age documents. Her "significant other" did not want her to work at night so he ratted her out. Even though the license in question was real (her sister's), I was fired for the infamous, "We gotta give the liquor board somethin'...you should have known...be a better mind reader...you stupid so and so" clause.
- I worked for a disturbed man who would remove from inventory all of the Grand Marnier, along with cases upon cases of beer every weekend for his personal consumption. Of course, he would then routinely press for lower liquor costs from the business.
- I improved product cost percentages by implementing frequent inventory counts; and conversely, by eliminating frequent inventory counts in favor of increasing staff trust and individual job ownership.

- I was chief therapist *and* operations manager for two warring factions. The wife of one partner did not like the other partner; the partnership ebbed and flowed depending on how much grief the first partner received at home.
- I lost an entire Friday night of sales because a strapping young man hoisted a keg over his head in the tap beer cooler and busted a fire sprinkler, triggering the loudest alarm you have ever heard. Subsequent pipe failures and flooding ensued. (The water shut-off valve was located in a chained off part of the shopping center.)
- I have increased productivity by hiring more servers and reducing section sizes at poorly performing properties; and strangely enough, I have increased productivity by downsizing service staffs and increasing section sizes at poorly performing properties.
- I have witnessed full diapers left on tabletops by parents and upper plate dentures in water glasses left by seniors. (These are not appropriate tips!)
- I maintain that menu design is as important as new recipe development, but neither will produce more long-term profits than proper daily security procedures, product preparation to par levels, proper portioning, and waste tracking.
- I have wrapped dozens of hands cut by shards of glass and searched for missing fingertips on four occasions.
- On two occasions, bewildered and/or intoxicated guests have navigated straight to the ice machine and convulsively vomited, contaminating all fifteen hundred pounds of ice.
- On three occasions, the Heimlich maneuver has saved lives in my presence.
- I have increased profits by both opening stores for additional day parts and by reducing store operating hours.
- No fewer than twenty-five couples met while working for me and subsequently were married. Usually I was playing stupid not cupid. It is the "nature of Mother Nature" or so they all said to me when I could no longer ignore their (very frowned upon) work-time hook-ups.
- A female manager of mine, hesitant to intervene in a sexual romp taking place in a men's room stall, sent in a male busser

to break up the action. The busser was successful in getting the male to dismount and vacate the restroom, but when said busser returned to escort the female patron outside, Little Miss Down and Dirty invited him to take over where the other guy left off...and he did! (Was she unaware of the pause or simply unquenchable?) This was the only time any of us had to terminate an employee during intercourse. And yes, this is really a true story that happened in a casual dining restaurant.

- I have struggled mightily in my attempt to successfully coexist with health departments, zoning commissions, local signage boards, fire marshals, police officers, *ADA, PETA, INS, ICE,* IRS, landlords, equipment reps, repair services, pagans, vegans, husbands, wives, and moms and dads.
- I realized the tremendous need to become a resourceful collector of bartered services: design, public relations, wood refinishing, plumbing, city council schmoozing, hinge and lock, and so forth.
- I was not hired by a famous restaurateur for a *GM* job after he flew me to Los Angeles for an interview. His "guru" looked at a picture of me and did not like my aura. (They *really* gave me this as the reason.)
- I was not hired for a *GM* job because of my initial reluctance to shave off my beard. (Why did Uncle Wizney think that hairy faces scare little children? Hello!? Santa Claus, anyone?)
- I was hired for a *GM* job and when asked whether I would be willing to shave off my beard, I replied, "How about if I shave off half of it as a compromise?" The interviewer liked my brazen suggestion. (I intended to keep my mustache; he thought I was willing to shave right down the middle, half a face with hair and half without.)
- I was once hired as a *GM* specifically because I had worn cowboy boots to the interview (the interview was in Texas).
- I grew a ponytail and beat out two other candidates for a promotion. (I then looked more New York.)
- I cut off my ponytail and received a promotion. (I then looked more Midwest.)
- I have fired people for being insolent, inattentive, indifferent, and injurious. (They all seemed to feel as justified in their

actions as I felt in my response.)

- I have had store sales cut in half by unannounced city work projects and doubled by unexpected competitor closings.
- I have *never* met a budget that favored my potential bonus.
- I have been sweet-talked, petted, propositioned, poked, slapped, and slugged. Stop for a moment and imagine me *smiling* through all of the spit-talkers, hacking coughs, streams of vomit, and untold sneezes that were spewed forth by the teeming mass of sickness known as our guests (ew, but true). Helpful hint: When the music is too loud for polite conversation, turn your head so the germs go in your ear, not in your mouth.
- I have subdued a knife-welding employee and have dodged many attempts to harm my well-being, but I have not, as of yet, been shot. It is possible that on some occasions when I worked for myself I found it necessary to carry a gun to and from work when making scary night deposits (stupid and very risky!).
- I saved countless thousands of payroll dollars simply by ensuring that the right people clocked in and out on time.
- I denied entrance or service to respectable folks who were acting intoxicated and escorted boisterous troublemakers off numerous properties. (The cops on TV are right—a domestic disturbance is always the most dangerous, with rival gangs and ironworkers tied for a close second.)
- I have come to understand that even the best people believe that the lamest excuse is reason enough to miss a work shift.
- I never use a urinal in a public restroom, only lockable stalls—a lesson learned after being "cold-cocked" while taking a leak by the posse of a guest who had been asked to leave.
- I have conceived of numerous human resources, menu, marketing, and design solutions that were adopted companywide on a national level.
- I have given viable solutions for operational problems that never left the launching pad because of red tape, a supervisor's inattention/incompetence, or blind organizational denials that any problems even existed.
- I also had a bunch of dumb ideas that rightfully wilted away

once they saw the light of day.

- I am the same person who was called the "best of the best" when working for like-minded people and deemed "an irascible cuss" when working for others.

Meeting topic:

Grab a handful from the above list and start a conversation, with an eye on teaching the right thing to do when faced with disturbing scenarios.

I have worked for the complicated, the confused, the happy, and the humble; I have also worked for completely broken crayons, addicts, and adolescent adults. But by far the worst of the lot are the perpetually angry, hold you down'ers—they sit atop my watch list, besting the criminal and the freak-flag flyers.

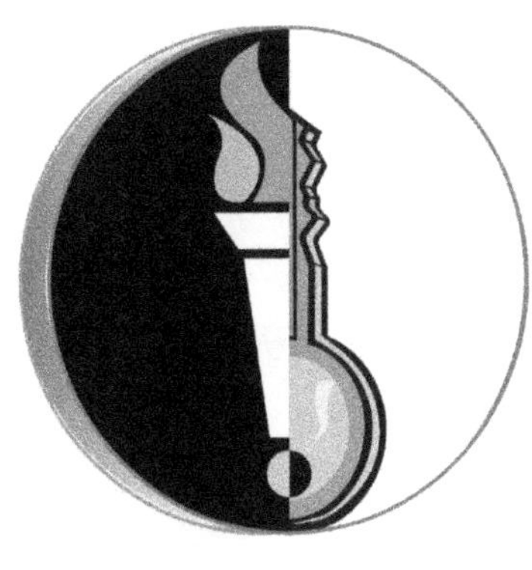

Chapter 12
Leadager Up!

Step up, hustle, let's go, move it! If you are a general manager who has just been given a new opportunity, the following will most certainly describe you:

- You have an adaptive and curious nature with a strong work ethic.
- You are consumer-trend aware, decisive, flexible, adventurous, energetic, and resistant to stress, with an aptitude for mechanical repairs.
- You are a persuasive personality, fanatical tribe-builder, thoughtful developer of talent, consummate networker, creative marketer, navigator of unforeseen circumstances, and master of practical business economics.

If not, you have some work to do because the unwritten expectation accompanying the *GM* position is that *in all areas, you will see and do what could and should be done.*

The first thing to get into your *GM*'s (*leadager*'s) head is that general management *is a different job* with distinctive boundaries, expectations, and benchmarks. You are not in "assistant land" anymore. You have been given responsibility to lead (a true action verb in my book) a store or property to success. You must begin day one with a clear understanding of how success will be measured. *Clarify and confirm these expectations.* Is this a "things are fine, just don't screw it up" maintenance situation? Or is it a "time to clean house, everybody goes" turnaround? Maybe you find yourself with a brand-new store

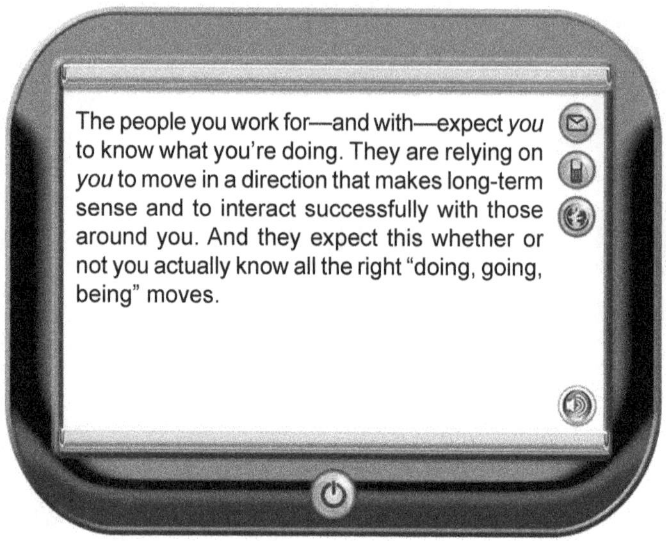

opening on which you can put your own imprint. Or you might be requested to add a few quick cosmetic changes (also known as lipstick) before a sell-off.

For each unique scenario, different approaches and solutions are required. However, there are a few classic moves to take into account when assuming ongoing operations:

- If possible, review the financial history of the new operation before you accept the position. Is there a downward or upward trend in sales? What are the expense reduction opportunities or sales increase possibilities?
- Can you pick your own co-*leadagers* or are you inheriting the A team—or zombies? This is important; selecting your own tribe is preferable.
- Make an unannounced visit to the unit as a customer. What was the experience like? What was lacking? What was exciting?
- Arrange to visit the unit when there are no other employees present (with the cleaning crew). Use all your senses. What is dirty? What smells bad? How are things stored? How are things maintained? Is any of the furniture, fixtures, and equipment (*FF&E)* in need of repair?
- Look at the schedules. Is the unit currently under- or over-staffed? What is the establishment's current reputation as an employer in its market area? Is it tough to hire good people? (There is always a war for good talent, but you will surely

fail if you don't have enough "somebodies" to start out with.)

- Get a map of the area. Draw 1-, 3-, and 5-mile circles around your store and personally drive those neighborhoods. Note the highest-trafficked streets, your direct competition, and businesses that could be potential promotion partners.
- Go to city hall, the local library, or your favorite online search engine and research the history of your area. Where is the closest retirement community, resort, high school, college? Are there any local heroes, festivals, or traditions?

These exercises will allow you to formulate an opinion about which way the wind is blowing for the property and how to prioritize your plan.

The "immediate betterment" moves that you can make will (should) be glaringly obvious. However, you will need a transition, or bridge, from the past to your arrival. You represent change and people are conditioned to like their habits. They may be reticent and suspicious of you, regardless of your intent toward individual performance and business improvements. The quicker you are able to induce/incent the tribe to bend toward your new direction, the better your chances for success.

One approach that might allow you to leverage your "window of arrival" to your advantage is to provide a fresh forum for the voices within the group. Most hourly employees believe they do not have any ability to influence business direction. You can successfully alter this perception by holding one-on-one meetings with the majority of the key players. You are required to *listen* (and consider) their answers to the following classic business questions.

In order to make our business better:

1. What should we *stop* doing around here?
2. What should we *start* doing around here?
3. What are your *favorite* things that we do around here?
4. If you owned this business, which *tribe members* would you *clone* to have more of the best people?
5. What needs to be *cleaned, repaired,* or *replaced?*

You will now have three lists: the one your supervisor gave you, your own, and the tribe's. Combine the items, assign (weighted) values, and prioritize them. You now have an action plan for the near future.

(If you are really on your "A game," you will periodically ask the above questions of your *guests.*)

After the plan is solidified, you will need to hold a group meeting. The best transition meeting I ever attended, successfully shifted control and focus from the past into the present. It opened with the following introduction:

> "Welcome, and thanks for coming. There are many people here who have worked at XYZ store for a long time. We want to take this opportunity to thank you for all your hard work. Please stand up if you have been with the group for longer than six months. (Applause) There are some new faces that have not been here quite as long. Let's welcome them as well. (Applause)
>
> "We have gathered here today to speak about the changes we are facing. Change is not easy. In fact, it can be very hard. But, as with most things, change is inevitable. People move away, people get married, people have kids, and we all, hopefully, grow older. Businesses change as well—new customers, new menus, new uniforms, and new policies.
>
> "I would like you to think of this business as a bus that has taken us all on a trip. What a trip! Some good times, some bad times, but now we have pulled off at a rest stop. We can all get out today and stretch our legs. We can see the whole horizon. Take a look back at where we came from. Now go ahead! Look at all the possible places we can go from here. You should know that while we were walking around, the bus driver unloaded all of our luggage. Right there, next to our bus are all the bags that you have packed while working together—quibbles, rudeness, gripes, grumbles, friction, and fog.
>
> "There is, however, a little hitch in our travel plans. *The place to which this bus is headed has room for everybody, but it does not have room for everybody's old baggage.* We can't get there if we are all hanging onto what was done or said in the past. This baggage simply represents too much weight to get us over the next hill.
>
> "We need to focus on the future and that is what the rest of today will be about."

Which business goals are worth shooting for? Well, just like people, businesses need regular health checkups. The health of hospitality operations falls into three categories:

1. Thrivers
2. Strivers
3. Survivors

A *thriving* operation looks like…

A sparkling business! Guests can always count on the excellent consistency and quality of the food, beverage, service, and spirit/tempo provided by the operation. The guests feel as if they are the most important thing in the building—as if they are the winner of each and every transaction. The balanced employee rhythm between personality and professionalism is visible. The relationship-building skills of the tribe are superlative. Guests actually pass by competitors to visit this establishment. People proudly invite their family and friends to this operation.

The staff feels like a million bucks. They are treated with civility and held accountable to expectations, yet are empowered to do the right thing. They have the tools, training, and support to do their best. It's about more than just the money; they willingly share in the responsibility to create a great guest experience. This is because of the high level of "fit" and "buy-in." The tribe holds a clear understanding of how their roles contribute to the outcome, and not surprisingly, they are motivated to help each other exceed expectations. They would invite their friends/family/competitors to work here.

Leadagers are focused on making every moment count. They are clearly aligned with a system that is healthy and targeting the growth of all. They have a hardy supply of skill, stamina, and wisdom. They work at identifying daily goals and are actively clearing the path to success. These *leadagers* support victories with celebratory "pump-ups." Work challenges are viewed as opportunities to stretch and grow. They are committed to building successful business results by fostering successful business relationships. Sales and profits are on the rise.

The unit looks fresh and clean, regardless of its age. Its sparkle shows off the "store-proud" activities of the people who work here. Through their outreach efforts and business practices, this store has become a welcome addition to the community.

There is positive word-of-mouth power in the marketplace about this property. A *thriving operation* is taking market share from its competitors. The end result is magnetic. *They are attracting new business by the way they have handled their old business.* Good job!

A *striving* operation is …

A notch below the aforementioned *thrivers,* but things are nonetheless on the rise. There is still unmet potential in some performance areas. The level of service, food, and beverage satisfies most of the guests. The spirit can be seen frequently but not always. A consistent sense of urgency is lacking and the highest standards are rarely exceeded. The staff is not stridently focused on the guest perspective, but the guest feels that with some effort, they can get a medium amount of attention. This property might be on the list of places to go, but it is not at the top.

On most days, the staff feels as though they are on the right track. Some difficulties exist, but they are fewer in number than in the past. The tools, training, and support are producing a movement toward doing the right thing at the right time. In terms of the fit, there are more "get its" than "don't get its." Recently, the group can count more wins than losses. "Buy-in" is not a hardship.

Leadagers are working on a solid plan. There are established goals that seek to close performance and productivity gaps. The full impact of business relationship-building has yet to be fully leveraged. Commitment to success is high, but execution doesn't always meet expectations. Sales and profit targets are achievable, but one or the other usually falls short.

This property has had recent improvements in *FF&E,* and repairs are made in a timely manner. At this point, not all the major "to-be-fixed" issues have been addressed. This store is turning its talk of being a good neighbor into action but has not fully turned the corner.

This business is giving its stronger competition a "run for the money," but market share is only taken from weaker competition.

This unit is striving for more. If it continues in this direction, the best is yet to come for all parties. But there is still a ways to go. (These types of stores are also called the "*Yes, but…*" operations.)

A *surviving* operation...

Is just trying to hang on. It is plagued with consistency problems between shifts, depending on whether a *leadager* or "wannabe" is working. Repeat business built through frequent, positive guest experiences is not a reliable commodity. Apathy is an issue and is felt by the guests. Standards, spirit, tribal unity, and quality are merely concepts without a connection.

The staff is self-absorbed and disassociated with the business at hand. Most requests to put forth a strong effort are met with reluctance. "Why should I try? So and so doesn't" is a common refrain. A very weak "big picture" understanding undermines most efforts. The "fit" and "buy-in" are out of balance. Requests for any "above and beyond" involvement is met with anger, laughter, or silence.

Meeting topics:

- How do you clarify and confirm expectations of your performance?
- Pick any of the five questions from the beginning of this chapter.
- What would your first moves be if you became GM?
- How would you describe a thriving operation?
- Have you ever written down the ideal guest experience at your establishment from start to finish? If you have not, how are you going to measure and track improvements in your system?

The management is mistaking activity for accomplishment. Values are in the background and quickly submerged if control is tested. Exceeding guest expectations is not the highest priority. In fact, getting people to work on time is an all-consuming effort. Systems are not being maximized and policies are overutilized. Managers tend to display a high level of frustration.

Cleanliness and organization are issues. Repairs are running behind and the unit is aging at an accelerated rate. Connecting beyond the four walls is rarely done and the community at large is not impressed with this operation as a neighbor. This business may be used out of convenience, but it is not a happy choice for the customer. Sales and profits are a struggle. *This store is losing market share and the long-term health of the business is in question.* It is *surviving,* but for how long?

In summary, this "working from the same page" technique is a massive and ongoing undertaking. Start early and refresh often.

These snapshots are provided as a guide. If you discuss the ideal "thriving" vision with your new tribe, you will initiate a valiant attempt to get everyone to share your vision (of what good and bad joints look like).

Chapter 13

Cooking With Gas

The time has come for me to break it to all of you newly promoted *GMs* (*leadagers*): Your past efforts and achievements may have been good enough to get you this job, but they are not good enough to produce long-term success in your new one. Don't allow yourself to be fooled by your own record. A horse and a jockey both run the same race, but neither is supposed to do the job of the other. So it goes with *leadagers*—and with assistant managers and *GM*s. I am here to tell you to expect more, more, more—more time demands, more problems, more paperwork, and more planning.

You must realize you cannot physically do every job, yet you will be judged by the performance of the entire operation. To become a successful *leadager*, you must become a master of motivation, a dedicated "delegator," and a monster about follow-up and follow-through.

Motivation is usually internally defined and externally influenced. People do things off the cuff that may or may not be good for them (also called being impulsively shortsighted). They may be working toward long-term goals (also called being driven), but all you really need to deal with is the following:

As your tribe is tested by the grind and as they begin to show their true selves, your job is to convince and persuade the strongest players to stay the longest, making sure that the "us" (the responsible, hard-working, smart, and caring ones) outnumber the "them."

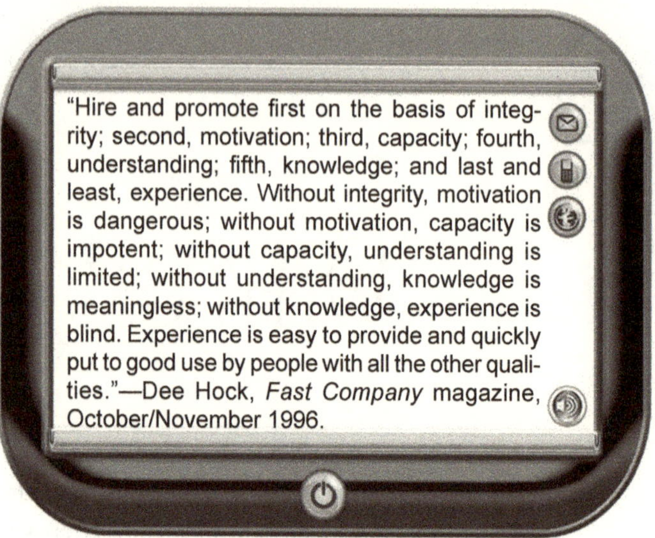

POSITIVE DIFFERENCE MAKERS

People may say they work for the company whose name is on the paycheck, but it has been shown that on a daily basis what they really do (or don't do) is driven by the *leadagers* they see the most. So what can you *really* do to make a positive difference?

- Know what you are doing—bring success; it breeds belonging.
- Connect the dots—be upfront about what each job requires and provide the why-dos, the how-tos, and not just the must-dos.
- Provide fair pay—a clear path to more money is one of the most impactful motivators you can provide.
- Provide fair play—a level playing field in regards to the rules, regulations, accountability and sensibility.
- Give 'em a voice—maybe the tribe won't get to vote on every item, but you can surely find a way for interested parties to become involved.
- Share what's in your head—your industry knowledge should be shared to help other people reach common goals.
- Celebrate strong performances—otherwise, they will think you are too "busy" for them or too stupid to know it when you see it.
- Use emotional restraint—walk away when tempted to "lose it, snap, or go ape." Everyone gets rattled; "teachable moments"

abound when you "unrattle" in a positive fashion. Clear your head and make decisions about courses of action outside the heat of the kitchen battle.

Delegation is not hard; avoiding abdication is. You can't release yourself from the outcome when you lead a tribe. The simple yet time-consuming approach is to break the work down into pieces and assign various parts to your fellows, according to their strengths, developmental paths, or areas of accountability. You must rigorously follow up with each according to their assigned responsibilities. If you lose track of their assignments/deadlines, it is tantamount to saying that it was not worth doing in the first place.

Try creating a mock manager (or *leadager,* if you now dare to be so bold) duties list, as if you were drafting a mock department schedule. The goal is to develop a duties checklist that, over time, reflects the true nature of the effort that must be undertaken to give your operation the best possible chance for success. (If it is good enough for NASA, it is good enough for you.)

MOCK MANAGER DUTY LISTS

Manager 1

- Kitchen schedule Tuesday @ 4pm
- Food inventory Sunday @ 12pm
- Food orders as needed
- Maintain food purchase journal
- Bread order
- Small wares order
- Code and input food invoices
- Update menu recipes
- HVAC/refrigeration maintenance schedules
- Kitchen department weekly meeting
- Kitchen training validations and timely reviews

Manager 2

- Bar schedule Tuesday @ 4pm
- Bar inventory Monday @ 6:00am
- Bar orders, as needed
- Maintain beverage purchase journal

- Code and input beverage invoices
- Standardize beverage menu recipes
- Bar department meetings
- Validation of bar training and timely reviews
- Interior signage
- Cleaning crew follow-up

Manager 3

- Server schedule Tuesday @ 4pm
- Host-bus-expo schedule Tuesday @ 4pm
- Linen order
- Service staff training validation and timely reviews
- Service department meetings
- New hire paperwork
- Menu-crayon-mint ordering
- Light bulb ordering-maintenance
- Point of sale (POS) paper-credit card-printer ribbon ordering
- Patio maintenance
- Host stand organization
- Safety program update

General manager

- Manager schedule Tuesday @ 4pm (two weeks out)
- Weekly manager meetings
- Manager development
- Daily cash reconciliation and bank deposits
- Weekly P&L reconciliation
- Cigarette order (if still legal)
- Payroll and reconciliation
- Local marketing plan
- Birthday and anniversary program for employees
- All-staff meetings once per quarter
- Sales forecasting
- Budget compliance
- Office supplies
- Purchase journal reconciliation
- Productivity tracking

- Shopper report/comment card/complaint/follow-up
- Credit reports

All managers

- Daily communications log book
- Open and close checklists
- End-of-shift checkout sheets and tip declaration
- Product quality line checks shift by shift
- Guest count log by historical hour
- Preventative equipment maintenance
- Monitoring prep-par-break-waste sheets
- Employee files and incident reports
- Accident reports
- ...and anything else that fits your gig

You may know this stuff like the back of your hand, but this is an attempt to get the whole enchilada out of your head and into the hands of the people who will make or break your success. *The newest managers might not be aware of the vast responsibility requirements. The veterans need to know how you prioritize the work.*

Next stop on your performance grid is the highly challenging task of increasing hourly tribe/team performance. I favor *pocket priority cards*. For each hourly department, create a card that fits into each person's pocket and make it mandatory to carry it while working. The cards include the company/store mission and values, plus a checklist of actions that make up a good shift. This becomes the heart of your daily pre-shift dialogue/quiz, allowing you to provide discussion points and answers to questions.

Pocket Priority Cards

Server priority card

- Did I clock in on time—ready to go?
- Am I aware of today's promotions and specials?
- Did I follow proper service sequence for each table?
- Did I use menu knowledge in action? (The goal is for you to know so much about our items that if the guest has you, they don't need a menu!)
- Did I recommend any of our best items?

- Did I ensure that all products served were up to our standards?
- Did I revisit in two bites or two minutes?
- Did I do my side work throughout my shift?
- Did I thank all my guests for the visit?
- Did I help a tribemate who was "weeded"?
- Did I practice full-hands in, full-hands out of the kitchen?
- Did I "own" any guest complaints until they were resolved?
- Did I inform the manager on duty (*MOD)* of any maintenance, quality, or guest issues?
- Did I learn six new guest names today?
- Did I set up the next shift for success?

Shift manager priority card

- Did I arrive early and plan my shift?
- Did I check the communications log?
- Did I use my checklists?
- Are we prepared for today's functions/promotions?
- Is my shift fully staffed, in uniform, and in proper personality?
- Did I conduct an informative and motivational pre-shift meeting?
- Did I make line/spec/plate checks at least once an hour?
- Did I make 80 percent or better table visits?
- Did I learn six new guest names this shift?
- Did I do three things to increase sales or decrease expenses this shift?

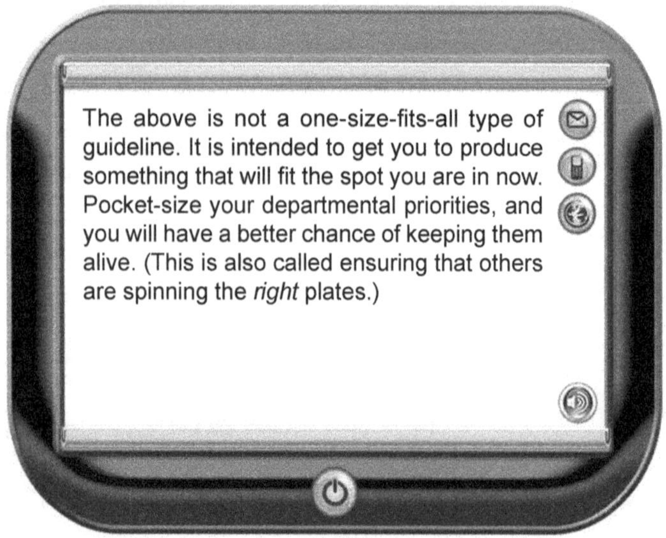

- Did I observe five cash handling transactions or complete a mid-shift cash drawer audit?
- Did I "coach-up" any poor performers?
- Did I have safety and security at "top of mind" during the shift?
- Did I own any guest issue until it was positively resolved?
- Did I learn something *factual, practical,* or *tactical* today?
- Did I set up the next shift for success?
- Were my decisions mission/values–based and did I endeavor to lighten someone's load?

FIRST FIXES FIRST

Top line/gross sales pressure for your establishment is inevitable. Weak sales may be the reason you have been given this opportunity. Strong sales are notoriously hard to maintain year-round, and you might have started out in the "valley." So what's the ticket out? Well, it is not for me to tell you, what with me sitting here and you sitting there. You are the one being paid to make the "firing line" decisions, but I *can* tell you what I have done in similar circumstances.

The best "first" sales move is always to make sure that your current guests are getting their money's worth. *Are the establishment's actions meeting or exceeding its words? Is the unit operationally succeeding?* If not, that is *the first fix.* (Slow ticket times; hot food served cold; cold food served warm; poor quality product; lousy service; dirty, smelly, or overall way too icky-sticky.)

Never attempt to get new guests to try a "we're working on it" experience. With that said, you might think I'm asking you to bear down until you can produce perfection. Not so. Just be able to back up your mission/values and standards/specs.

Guests' "hate it" card

- Poor phone etiquette
- Slow greeting
- Acting indifferent/unfriendly toward guests
- Dirty, smelly, unkempt uniforms
- Waiting for unbussed tables/unopen sections
- Soiled and sticky tables, counters, or surfaces
- Broken and/or ripped furniture or fixtures
- Lack of product knowledge

- Poor timing on delivery of food or beverage
- Dirty and/or out of stock utensils
- Auctioning of plates during delivery
- Receiving the wrong order
- Poor quality product
- Improper product temperature
- Foreign objects in food
- Noxious odors from bars, drains, or sewers
- Dirty/unstocked bathrooms
- Tribemates not washing their hands after a bathroom visit
- Slippery floors
- Visible clutter or disorganization
- Slow to ring or deliver a check
- Theft by overcharging
- Audible complaining or vulgarity by the tribe within earshot of guests
- Managers not interacting with guests
- No ownership of or positive resolution to problems
- No "thank you" or invitation to return
- Indecipherable hours of operation
- Unsafe parking lot

All of the above are common knowledge. The uncommon practice is for you to actually develop a system or habit to eliminate each of the aforementioned items from ever occurring in your establishment.

Marketing Simplicity

After resolving any/all of these glaring operational issues, the next two moves are intended to attract more patrons and to get the existing patrons to spend more money. Any discussion about increasing the top line or driving sales leads to the topic of marketing, which has evolved into a highly-analytical, pseudo-scientific discipline. I have always strived to accomplish the very things I was taught in a dry-as-chalk college class.

Attract attention, create interest, manifest desire, and induce action to increase sales. It is a simple formula that successfully predates all the current "must-do" marketing fads. All transactions are more memorable with customized service. All grizzled *leadagers* know that every sundae needs a smile and a cherry on top.

If you don't have any marketing shackles, that is, if the company is not directing your store's every marketing move, then I have a suggestion for you: *Ride the tide in the direction it is already moving.* This is also known as collaborating, co-promoting, piggybacking, and generally making it easier on yourself.

All over the world people are sweating and stewing about how to increase sales of their products (some of which you sell). Just imagine how much brain power is focused on advancing their prospects. You can use this fact to your advantage. Train yourself to identify where your needs and their needs intersect and then request the use of their resources (money) for the use of your snail/e-mailing list, special event partnerships, access to your parking lot, menu placement, and so on. ("What in the world can I do for you fellas and what can you do for me?")

Always begin your advertising adventure with an annual marketing/sales calendar you cobble together from the store's historical data and current trends. Start the assembly in the month of August to have it ready before January. Include holidays, three-day weekends (those Sunday nights usually produce more traffic), major sporting events, seasonal sales shifts, community festivals, and "in-service days" (i.e., when the schools are not in session).

Then layer in your purveyors' special promotions, selected dates for menu changes, seasonal beverage shifts, and any of the silly-somethings that you want to take advantage of (i.e., New Year's Eve, Valentine's Day, Mardi Gras, St. Patrick's Day, Secretary's Day, Cinco De Mayo, Mother's Day, Father's Day—always a bust for me, store anniversary/birthday party—always a winner, back to school, Oktoberfest, or even the national gift card months of November and December).

The main reason to do this work is to avoid undertaking a major effort for every marketing possibility that shows up at your door. If you build a comprehensive calendar and then trim down your selections to the ones that best fit your situation, you will put more muscle behind fewer choices. This way you will be exercising more control of your resources and possibly your fate. This should help you to plan in advance the entire coming year, rather than scrambling from month

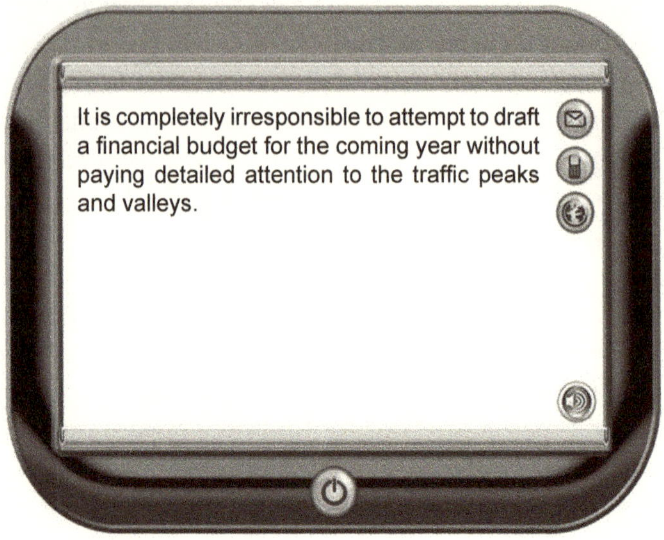

to month. It will give you a chance to train/educate and enlighten the tribe/crew as to what you are trying to do.

The above is the most direct route to establishing interesting and unique traditions at your particular unit. (Successfully executed traditions equals repeat business.)

Rules of marketing momentum

1. The first rule of hospitality marketing is to produce something worth talking about, also known as "signature items," "differentiation," "authentic-ness," or putting your best foot forward. (Make sure you can consistently "pull this off" before you start blabbing about it!)
2. The second rule is never have your tribe be confused or unable to articulate what your special, service style, promotion, or feature presentations are all about (they are the *facilitators* of the potential ideal experience for the guest).
3. The third rule is to leverage "user-friendly" as far as you possibly can (web-based reservations, social networks, delivery, curbside pick-up, frequent purchase rewards, community involvement, easy to operate/read menu, flexible menu sub-

stitutions, etc.; and maybe even trimming the tree that is partially covering your store signage).

4. The fourth rule is to nudge (without being pushy) for extra sales that can be coaxed from the wallets/purses of the visitors you already have. Don't ignore the specials or "combos" that will bring you the best margins. I once asked a server who was beating the pants off everyone else in a "side salad" promotion what magic he was using to produce such great results. He said, "I just try to remember to ask everyone if they want a side salad with their order; it's only $4.75." Oh, I see; asking for extra sales in a nice, informative way produces more sales.... Really? Duh!
5. The fifth rule is that there is no "one best way" to market your establishment. The time and place you occupy will indicate whether you will be better suited for one method over another. Glossy postcard mailings, TV, radio, parking lot inflatables, newspaper/magazine ads, web pages, networking, coupons, "four walls first," text messaging, viral, spiral, pyro, and simple word-of-mouth all have true believers.

Meeting topics:

- Would your guests say that your location lives up to its promises?
- How do you ensure follow up and follow-through?
- What is the difference between delegation and abdication?
- How do you chop the workload into manageable bites?
- How do you keep the purposeful intent and priorities fresh and alive?
- Is your in-house training program the very best that you can make it?
- Are you an advertiser, a marketer, or a relationship builder?
- What annual traditions are alive and well in your store?

The best ways to evaluate worthwhile efforts over wasted efforts is never to undertake any advertising without clear data that tracks the expenses versus the number of visits/sales that have actually been

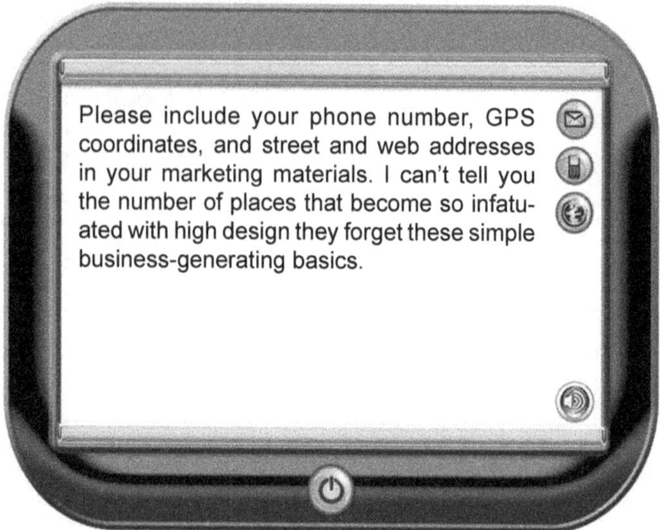

generated—your *ROI.* Never take part in a promotion that doesn't raise your profile with your target market and never do charity work unless it comes from your heart.

And so, you will have to slog through your choices like the rest of us. However, even with all those rules, I have one last thought: Never underestimate the power of supplying professional business cards to all key tribemates.

Chapter 14

Reality Check, Please!

Okay, you're starting to feel like you're really rolling. But not so fast! Right in the middle of your daily battles a "top dog" comes up and says, "We're not dropping enough money to the bottom line. We must do better!" What's the story? You cleaned up the place and things are definitely running smoother. Sales are on the rise, but you still have someone breathing down your neck about the bottom line numbers?

Yep! That's the way that it is! This *is* a business, after all, and whoever owns it is feeling pressure from banks, partners, stockholders, "significant others," and/or bookies who all view themselves differently than you do. The owners often believe they are the pragmatic ones (and they secretly harbor the belief that if you were better with money, you would own something, too). You, however, are working in an upside-down world of part-timers that is filled with immature distractions and operational interruptions; consequently, the owners may discount your opinions on the achievable/ideal bottom line figure. (Okay, maybe only 60 percent of your supervisors will think that ill of you.)

It doesn't matter what it *took* to achieve the profit you produced, they only want to know what you will *undertake* to deliver *more.* "Real" business people know that a dollar lost is hard to recapture and they act accordingly.

All of this may strike you as though senior management (stock holders/owner's wife) is expecting too much. There might be a similar version of the following rant ricocheting around in your head: "Enough with the unrelenting directives and threats about urgency and the simplistic focus on penny-pinching! Aren't they completely overlooking what we have accomplished here? Don't they get how far we have come?"

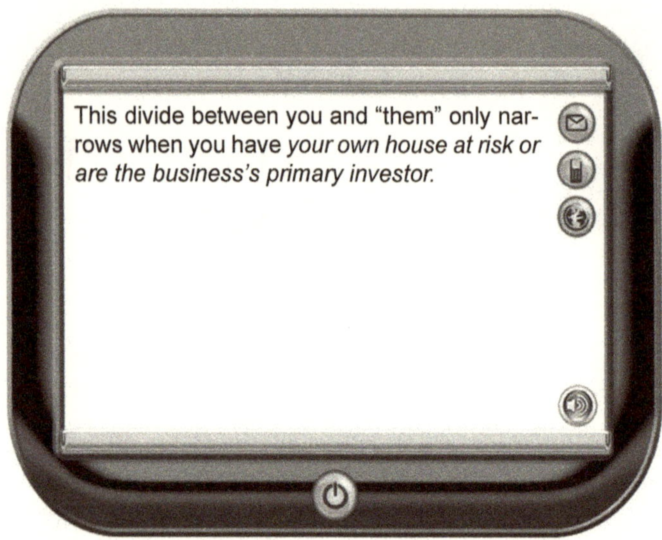

To all of the owners, bankers, and bookies out there, one quick word of caution: Robbing the future to further line the pockets of the present is not a course of action that will guarantee longevity. (Quick, go read about golden-egged geese!)

To all of the managers under the crushing thumb of "Now, dammit, now!"—directives focused on improving the bottom line—one quick word of caution: If you aren't making this happen, your bosses are already looking for somebody who will.

COLLECTIVE EFFORT

So what do you do? Well, the master *leadagers* take it as a personal challenge that can reveal itself in the following four ways:

1. The lame but sometimes wise, "I have no future here. I better get another job."
2. The overreactive but sometimes correct, "I'll show 'em. I can wring as much money out of this son of a gun as anybody."
3. The very rare, yet highly confident, "Back off! You hired me to run this place and it's gonna take some time to do it right. When it's right, you'll get your money and more."

4. The practical, and usually applicable, "Y'urrr right, we can always get better."

At all times it will be in your best interest not to be overwhelmed by "bottom line" pressures—they will *always* be there. The need to "make more money" is rightfully the nature of the capitalistic beast. It is a far better use of your energy to focus on the things that you actually have a chance to change than it is to chafe against this absolute.

I'm sure some comparisons have already been tossed in your direction (e.g., performance is not as good as last year/xyz store/previous *GM).* Now is the time to raise your periscope and uncover industry or organizational financial information to use as near-term benchmarks.

Target your weakest cost areas as compared to budget and chart a course to break into the top five or top ten list (figured in percents) within your group of stores or industry averages. (Helpful hint: Go after the biggest chunks of dollars first—labor, food, beverage, and so on.) As experienced by everyone in a modern competitive economy, you will have to increase your productivity (same number of people or systems working harder or smarter) or decrease your expenses (reduction in people, places, or things that cost you money) while increasing, or at a minimum, maintaining gross revenues.

There are a hundred ways to get this done, but none will be achievable in the world of hospitality without clear goals, strong systems, and disciplined efforts from the tribe. Of course, you have all lived through the annual cost-cutting plans, marketing push, or new menu rollout that targets "getting from here to there."

You can't get there (the achievement of your targeted goals) from here (wherever you are starting from) unless there is alignment (most everyone working off the same page) about where here is (in what direction we are currently headed) and which there (what the priorities are) matters the most!

Everyone who faces the challenge of leading a group of people is dealt the same set of basic challenges: banding together instead of splitting apart, putting forth some kind of solid communal effort, and actually accomplishing/achieving targeted goals.

If you have not already done so, perhaps now is the time to consider how this gets accomplished in the "real world" (i.e., outside of the hospitality/service industry). How in the heck have leaders throughout history gone about the business of taking diverse groups of people and persuading them to buy into the program so profoundly they collectively agree to pull in the same direction?

They start with a simple framework, the definition of good and bad, success and failure. Within their own context, they outline the good things that can come to those who do well and the bad things that can happen to those who do poorly.

Recognize and reward those who follow the path and discipline or remove those who insist on moving in the opposite direction. Throw in an appeal to commit to something that is bigger than one's self (group identity or common goals), stay consistent with your focus on what the "ideal wins" look like, and don't get sidetracked by the little things. Leaders also create guides, handbooks, or interactive videos as training tools and also send out a few exceptional emissaries (trainers) to "walk the walk" of the vision.

Hmm...this sounds a lot like big business, religious, political, or military undertakings. That's right—the same tried-and-true methods can be used in your organization because no one has come up with a better way to "bring people together" (albeit with a little tweaking since you are not offering survival training or revealing a path to save their soul).

You are living your professional life under this construct whether you know it or not, but most people under managementship pressure fall to the *temptation of dictation*, that is, "things to do" or "marching orders." Yet telling people what to do is the smallest and most limiting part of a successful *long-term* strategic program of positive change.

Although it is of paramount importance to choose the right set of financial or operational goals, it is *equally essential* to be *crystal clear* about the purpose and overarching goals that are being driven forward through completion of the assigned tasks. Both must be attached to a clear link to the self-interest of fellow tribe members. ("What's our cut? Hey, bub, *what* do we get outta this?")

What follows are some dark and light examples of "linkage" attempts that have been thrown my way over the years. I revisit them exactly as they were stated to me.

The so-called "carrots":
"This will lead to more money for you."
"They don't believe in you, but I do."
"They had their time. Now it's our time to shine."
"I don't care what they taught you, my way is the right way."
"We are all in this together, it's us against the world, baby!"
"We are trying to do something special and we need your help."

The so-called "sticks":
"You're either with me on this…or you are done."
"You're as dumb as a stump. I dare ya to prove me wrong."
"You're going to have to take a step back until you get in step."
"We're just gonna have to keep beating you like a drum 'til you're tired of gettin' beat."

Obviously, some of the above did impact me in the short-term, but most did not allow me to feel connected to a bigger picture. If you don't have anyone else moving in the direction you wish to go, you will never get the results you seek. You must become a skilled enlister, enroller, and engager, drawing the tribe into your plan. *This is also known as creating buy-in, making meaning, or forming a connection.*

It's in the packaging, kiddo! Hot dogs and sausages are snouts, guts, and other *stuff.* Is this the best way to present your product? Not if you intend to make a sale. The same goes for forging a new direction, "sea change," or action plan.

A HOSPITALITY *LEADAGER'S* UNIVERSAL MISSION—*LIFT*[2]

The following is my well-traveled, professional managementship mission. It has been honed, tested, and positively received by numerous people with whom I have worked. I'm sharing it now to save time for those of you who never have spent a moment wrestling with this stuff (not to start a cult). Use this as a navigational tool for your tribe's new direction, or take the time to come up with one of your own design.

Lead—To manage myself into becoming an excellent contributor (act first, talk second), then add value by recognizing and transforming possibilities into realities.

Improve—If you continually contribute to making the

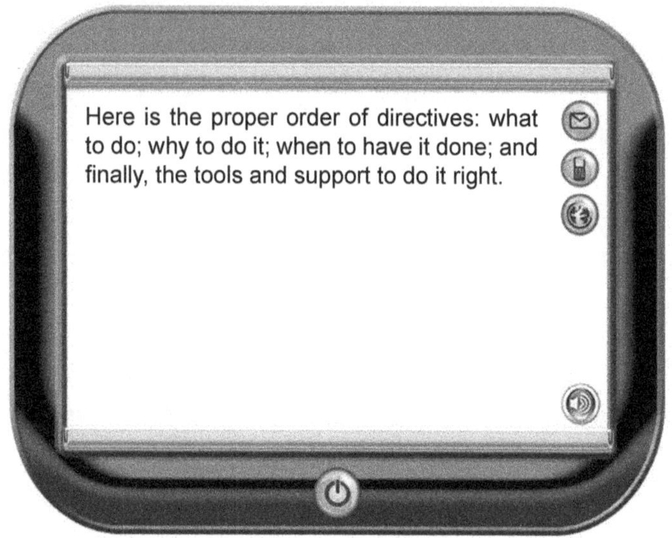

organization better, you will be ensuring the best possible future for everyone.

Focus—Apply all of your personal resources to the present business moment. This will provide the shortest route to exceeding expectations, a key competitive advantage.

Tribe—Actively promote a unifying culture that depicts "a clear path to wins" by utilizing shared legends, symbols, and totems. All of us can draw pride and strength from our connection to a positively unified effort.

Tenacity—Unassailable determination, an undeterred will. The simplicity of undeniable resolve. This is the single most important factor in any achievement.

LIFT^2's purpose:

* *LIFT* the performance of the business to sustainable successes.
* *LIFT* the experience of our guests beyond their money's worth
* *LIFT* the contributions of tribemates beyond previously conceived levels.
* *LIFT* the spirit of the surrounding community by our active involvement.

The following quotes provided me with the inspiration for *LIFT*:

"There are two kinds of people
On earth that I mean
There are the people who lift and
The people who lean."
—Ella Wheeler Wilcox

"There is a loftier ambition than merely to stand high in the world. It is to step down and lift mankind a little higher."
—Henry Van Dyke

Don't get me wrong. It is imperative to stop the cash from bleeding out of an operation and to rectify any other significant deviations from the ideal vision, but—and I must repeat myself here—*you cannot do it alone.*

I'm not suggesting that during a *fire* you have to stop to explain why fire is a bad thing. You just yell, "Everybody out!" And certainly during the crush of the rush you will issue more directives rather than stopping to engage in lengthy dialogues, but you have to follow up with "connectors" when you are attempting to grow and lead your people.

By now you have discovered you cannot just "wing it" when it comes to credibility. You earn trust and build respect and relationships one interaction/one decision at a time. Yes, you will encounter the sour apples, the disengaged, and the part-timer attitudes. But this is why you get paid the big bucks. Most people will listen to you and respond in a positive way, right? You are the credible one, aren't you? Remember when we discussed authenticity and credibility? Well, here is where the oil heats up in the pan; bring forth all your *leadager* savvy and start cookin.'

Giving orders or relying on positional power each and every time there is a challenge may be the norm in religion, politics, or the military; however, this approach won't be effective with hospitality tribes. If you are perceived as dumb or "bossy," they will quit on you. If you are too much of a friend, they will roll right over you. All great *leadager*s know it is the right move at the right time that gets you where you need to go. (Jeepers creepers—not that again!)

Some people seem to think that working on message delivery is unnecessary. With cement feet they proclaim, "Look, I'm just going to be me and people will just have to deal with it." Well, what if being you is too overbearing for the situation? What if your bear-like demeanor translates into being the micromanager everyone despises? What if being you is caught up in being an appeaser, and the work isn't being done because the tribe is taking advantage of you? And what do you think will happen if your boss despises your approach?

There are plenty of line employees who would rather work for a monster because they can consistently count on the reactions of that person. There are people who would rather work for a sweetheart because all chances of conflict are removed. However, being defined as either one of these extremes will likely put the brakes on your ascent to greater responsibility levels. You must wear many hats (assume the correct persona) when leading a tribe. You might have to "go against the grain" or be abrasive in the opposite direction of "who you are" to get things done.

Some of you may feel as if this focus on your "delivery" is not connected to slinging hash, putting butts in the seats, or booking rooms. But by cracky, you *are* concerned with building your "brand" as a *leadager*, aren't you? Billion-dollar, multinational brands are working hard every day to tailor their "message delivery" to a target audience.

The product of you, as a *leadager* professional is certainly worth your best consideration.

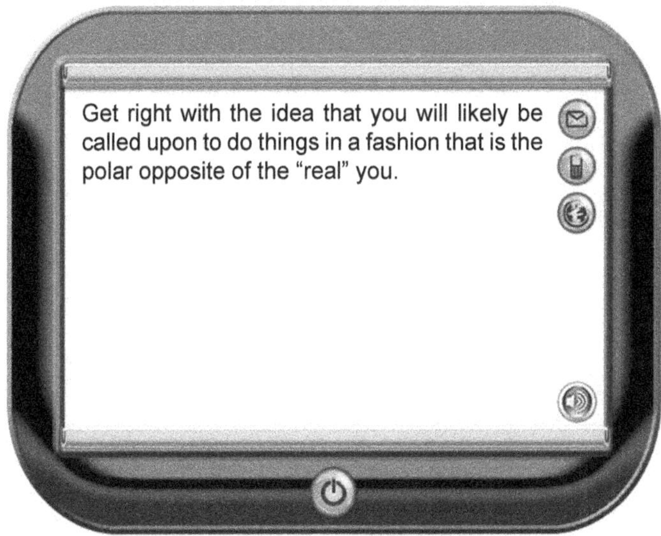

The right action at the right time (not always the way you would feel most comfortable) will most effectively address your problems. Any problem you face has two parts: (1) everything you can see or process, and (2) the course of action you take toward resolution.

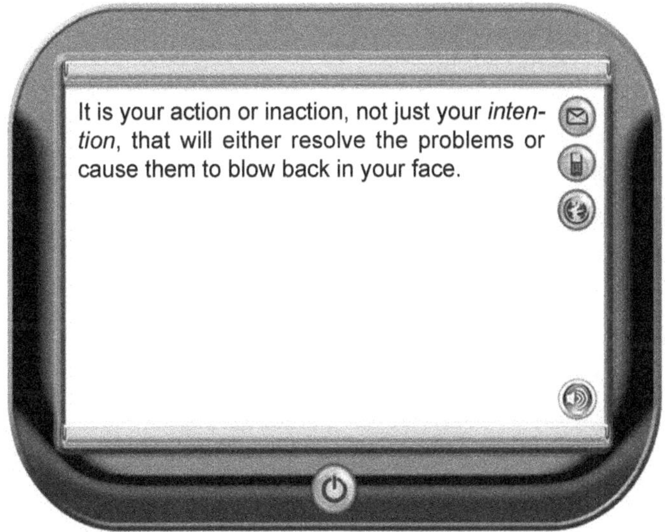

This is why organizations and owners place a premium on problem solvers rather than problem identifiers. ("You handled that nicely" as opposed to "Thanks for handing me that bag of snakes.") They are looking for *leadagers* who can fix the issue at hand and not end up creating bigger problems through their misguided approach. No one really wants to help you do the work of fixing the problems that clearly fall within your area of responsibility. They might empathize with you, or coach or counsel you about the matter, but most are reluctant actually to jump in and do the thing for you. (They usually have enough work of their own.)

Surround yourself with problem solvers—folks who have the spirit and personality to fix the stuff inside and outside of themselves. Many companies now use personality profiles or trait assessments as part of their new hire selection process. My advice is to use whatever tools, tests, fiery hoops, or voodoo charms that are at your disposal—and legally available—to increase your odds of hiring "the right fit."

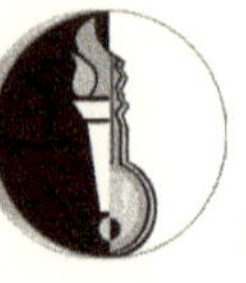

Meeting topics:

- Why are bottom-line discussions always at the top of our mind?
- Why does achieving financial goals take a collective effort?
- What are your best tools for reducing expenses or increasing productivity?
- Does your company/store have a mission? Do you use it to lift or lean?
- Do you practice your message delivery?
- How do you "make meaning" for others?
- Are you a problem identifier or a problem solver?
- Why don't (in most cases) intentions count for anything?

If you aspire to the top rungs of the responsibility ladder (again, read as: more money for you), then this has to become an area of ongoing self-awareness and effort. (Hopefully, you will consider the fact that I did not come to this particular realization overnight, but rather through years of professional dues-paying.) You see, the dishes or a steak can be "done," but true *leadager* work is never done. He or she is always seeking continuous personal and professional development. Through the combination of trial and error, stretching, and growing, one can develop the ability to carry heavier *managementship* loads and greater *leadager* responsibilities.

Becoming an accomplished *LIFT*-er is the short road to real professional legitimacy and relevance, two qualities that will serve you well throughout your life and career.

Chapter 15
Driving the Ownership Dream

I WAS ALL ALONE. A SINGLE RED WINE DROP on an all-white tablecloth would have felt more comfortable than I did. That I am still able to register a memory on this matter is a feat in and of itself since my brain was as sluggish as an old V8 engine on a frigid winter morning.

As I recall, it was about 7am. Shards of sunlight were slicing through a set of broken shutters, highlighting an impressive display of dancing dust. I had been flat out for about four hours. There I was, sprawled across the middle of a hardwood dance floor. My own snores had startled me awake, and I discovered myself to be half out of my sleeping bag. The woes of that dance floor were monumental—the greatest of which was having recently been the victim of a fury-filled, chainsaw-welding, destruction-bent human being.

Let's backtrack for a moment: Since my first foray into the hospitality industry, I had picked up distinct entrepreneurial leanings. Imagine this unusual circumstance: a person sniffing around in his early twenties, faced with the question—now what? What do I do for a living?

College had left me with virtually no marketable business skills, though I was rather confident in my skills as a waterbed salesperson at the time. For this I blame my own eclectic class selection and poor prioritization of study time. *("Chiquitas y cervesa?"* "Muy bueno!") So as the "out-of-the-box" thinker I envisioned myself to be, I went to the Yellow Pages. My goal—to read it forward and backward until it revealed to me a business I could start myself. (No one ever believes me when I regale this truth.) As I tackled the big yellow book, I made a ridiculously long list of all the potential possibilities I could pursue.

Then serendipity paid me a visit. While conveying my master plan to a runnin' buddy from way back who was working as a deejay, he mentioned that our old college hangout was for lease. Whoa! This was the old "hot spot." This place had it all—great music, foosball, pizza, pitchers, and piytchers, annnn pichaarrssth of beer (or so they tell me).

Dream fever set in. We could do this...and we could do that...all of it would be sooo great. "We could run our own place!" Ideas came to us in waves. Now I don't know anything about crack or crank, but I sure can tell you about mainlining dream juice. From the instant these ideas spilled out of our brains, it felt like we were sitting at the daily card game of the universe and had just laid down four aces and raked in the whole pot. We were completely entranced with the possibility of this dream becoming our future.

A half-baked plan began to take shape. First, get haircuts. Then borrow a nice car and suits that sorta fit. Meet with the landlord of the building and find out terms of the lease and the history of the space. Mister Landlord had a great deal of trepidation believing in two young "whippersnappers," but our ready-to-take-on-the-world enthusiasm won him over, if only on style points alone.

The previous tenants were troublemakers (his words) who had been late on their rent too many times. He had decided not to renew their lease. On the last night the previous tenants possessed the space, they decided to leave a message for the landlord in return for his booting them out. They exacted their measure of revenge on the facility itself. Anything they couldn't take with them that night became a target during a farewell party gone very wild.

Evidently things got quite out of hand. Cherry bombs went down the toilets. The walk-in cooler floor was splintered with an axe. The dance floor was mercilessly chain-sawed. The walls were covered with feces and the ceiling with remnant paint.

One area that took us by surprise was behind the bar. The beer taps were left open, empting the kegs onto the concrete floor, creating a river of hops, yeast, and alcohol. It was winter at the time so all the suds froze. With the arrival of warmer weather that spring, however, this mess had re-animated into layer upon layer of teeming stank, a wall-to-wall fungus carpet.

The property owner had taken one look at the awful mess and closed it up tight for over a year. Now he was trolling for tenants, and we rushed to take the bait. Other people had looked at the wanton destruction and had begged off the project we instantly dubbed "Mess Fest." We, on the other hand, remained smitten with the smack of dreams. All we could see was what lay on the other side of the contamination. First, a job for us of our own creation, then the pretentious "fringe bennies" that could come from being hospitality kings.

Quickly, maybe too quickly, we negotiated a lease option; we would give the landlord 5,000 dollars for a ninety-day option for the exclusive first shot at the lease. If we could not make a deal in ninety days, he would keep the money. Fortunately—or unfortunately—we only had five grand to our names at the time. Next, we cobbled together a rudimentary business plan from family advice and library books. (Take note: It is a very poor idea to have the first business plan you've ever read be the one you are writing.)

We were off, forming a sub-S corporation and selling stock to anyone who would have us. (*Please,* place a higher hurdle than that for potential shareholders to cross prior to joining your venture.) We funneled all cash for stock into a business account that created enough legitimacy for us to obtain the lease from the skeptical keyholder of our future.

What actually turned the trick in our favor with the landlord was paying (with promises of future free beverages) a friendly architecture student to render fantastic sight drawings of the interior and exterior of the establishment. Like most bootstrappers, we received emotional and financial support from our families, which to this day remains a debt we still owe, and that in reality we can never fully repay.

We also joined forces with the most genuinely ideal combination of talent in one person that one could ever hope to find on a startup team. Check this out: a competent and trustworthy attorney *with carpentry skills*. He had been recently divorced and had some time and money on his hands. Not only that, he saw potential in the venture and was bemused by our frenetic immaturity.

We saw in our heads something that did not yet exist and set about to turn that vision into reality. This was, and is, the driving force behind most business successes. Our vision became the true sustenance that we lived off during the birth of our business.

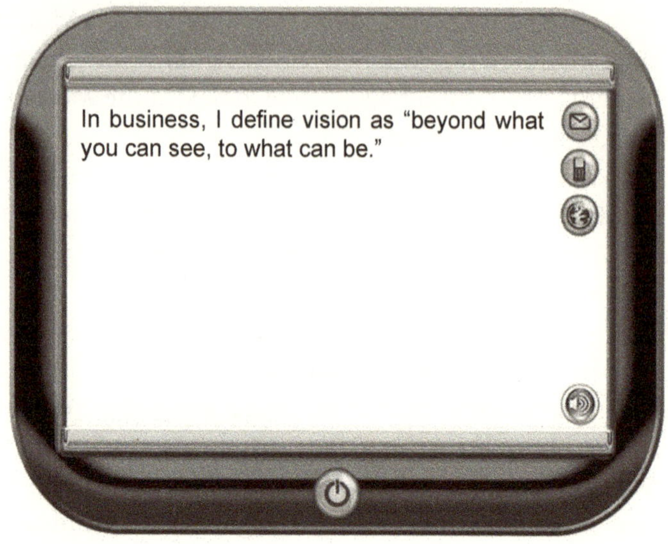

We stripped away everything that wasn't essential to our goal. I moved to the space above my parent's garage to eliminate paying rent, sold off my prized motorcycle, and ate on the fly. Sleep was an indulgent luxury. We didn't shop, party, play sports, or go to movies. Instead, we went to auctions to obtain used equipment for a song and analyzed competitors. Six months flew by as the three of us schemed, cleaned, bartered, and built. There was nothing else that mattered but driving the dream forward.

The force of my desire, willpower, and dedication to the task had surpassed all my previous endeavors. It was this positivity and drive that pulled my tired body over the many bumps in our road.

Passing the background checks, we were granted a liquor license. (If you ever dream of your name in lights—that is, having your own place with a liquor license—you had better avoid felony convictions.) At twenty-one, on the verge of twenty-two, I was the youngest person in the state of Colorado to be awarded the privilege of holding a liquor license.

Helpful ownership hints: If the plumber agrees to be paid in part with beer, consummate the arrangement after the job is finished. Never spray-paint a large indoor ceiling yourself; if you do, wear goggles and a mask. At the very least, don't wait until the over-spray adheres to your contact lenses and fills your mouth with paint to search out the finer points of ceiling painting. Additionally, make absolutely sure that your lease obligation is contingent upon your actually being granted a liquor license.

Early on, I had taken to sleeping in the building (see above) when I was too tired to drive home after yet another work-until-we-drop day. We were feeling the pressure to open and we were "crazy busy." The building, health, and fire departments were dealt with in our typical panic-and-naiveté-smothered-by-bravado style. (FYI: Seating capacity will be determined by your nimble depiction of seating/assembly areas/exit aisles and number of "johns.")

We had managed to hire our first employees. We seemed to lean toward those who were understanding enough to overlook our stammering and burrito-eating during their interviews. We learned that if you accept applications twenty-four/seven, you generate a lot more candidates. Many of our best players applied on their break or late at night after their shifts at other establishments.

As it has been said a thousand times—things can and will go wrong. Weird things pop up you didn't plan for or even think about. We were lucky, just plain lucky, that none of these things destroyed or derailed our dream. I drafted the following mantra for this period, which helped me stay focused:

To wish a dream *to life, your* desire *must be realized through* determination, discipline, *and* drive. *It is when you align your* decisions *and* dedication *with your actions that dreams manifest into destinations.*

I found this to be a mighty addictive spiritual lozenge!

LIFE SEASONING

Individuals who use their "all," and use it correctly, have accomplished many a success in business, athletics, and warfare. This, by the way, is the foundational reasoning smart folks use for hiring people who can draw from demonstrable military, sports, or previous business success.

All business leaders attempt to develop a "strategy" for their business, which simply comes down to the decisions they make to maximize all available resources to gain success, as they define it. If said leaders have had limited life experience, their strategies are usually limited in scope. If you get the chance in life to participate in something that fully challenges you and *demands* physical and/or maximum mental effort, sign up. This life "seasoning" directly adds value in a business environment.

Some experienced operators strategically start with a menu and build the establishment according to the equipment requirements. Some dream up the next big thematic trend and attempt to be the first to market a new idea. We were not the lowest-cost producers or the highest-quality mavens. We just used time, energy, skills, will, a spot of money, and cheaply purchased hard assets to reopen a place for the locals that had been shut down.

Having experienced a new business startup, I am here to tell you that if money solves a problem for you, then it is one of the easier tasks with which you will be presented. We did not have much money—all in, maybe enough to buy a small house. We coulda-shoulda invested in real estate with that money. We might have made out better, but where is the built-in job in that approach? (Is there anybody out there who would mind owning a house in Boulder, Colorado?)

We did more than most of the work ourselves, and like most of life's options, this was a trade-off. It came at the expense of our ability to raise our periscope beyond the task that was in front of our face. I wish we had taken the time to think about what it would be like after we opened, but we were inexperienced and truly consumed with the demands of opening.

I implore you to carve out time to plan and produce the materials needed for operations before you open for business. Training, marketing, accounting, and more were pushed to the back burner in our harried attempt to get the place open. (Use the many trade organizations or leaders in the field as resources to refer you to workable templates if you are carrying on without a clue.)

Over the years, I have met many proprietors who suffered the same ill-planned fate. When they should have been looking forward to a semi-smooth transition to opening, they were staring up from a dark gotta-get-caught-up hole.

As the days fell away, we were pressed to start generating cash for our survival. Prepare yourself for this threshold most small businesses cross. There are so many stories of dreamers who blow their wads before they open the doors and then have a couple of bad weeks, sending a year (or more) of work, plus their life savings, down the drain. We could easily have become a failure statistic because of our shoestring finances but luckily enough we were able to make money from day one. Not much but enough.

Embrace the concepts of operating capital and reserve capital. If you are building a budget now for a business plan, you must allocate money to carry on if things don't start off well. This can truly be the difference maker between success and failure.

Aside from talking to our neighbors, we had done minimal marketing. We picked a date three weeks out—after Christmas, at the start of the new year—to open our doors. Why open at the deadest time of the year? We did not know anything about retail cycles. It just seemed to us that college would be back in session and the remaining work could be finished by then. We advertised our coming grand opening with flyers on all community bulletin boards and in all the Laundromats we could find. We used a "coming soon" banner and mysterious come-hither teaser ads in the college paper classifieds, and solicited our more outgoing acquaintances to act as ambassadors by handing out grand opening invitations to all the party people they could find.

We were phone freaks (*not that kind*). We simply called anybody and everybody in the local phone book, told them about our

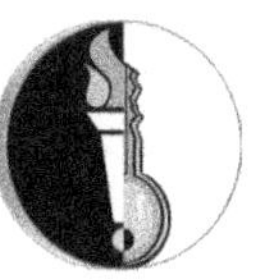

Meeting topics:

- How many business plans have you read, participated in preparing, or completed?
- Have you ever read or executed a business lease or purchase offer for commercial real estate?
- Do you have trusted and competent mentors/partners?
- Have you ever had a discussion with a building, fire, health, or zoning department official? A bank business loan officer, angel investor, or venture capital firm?
- In preparing to open your "baby," have you also prepared for operating life after opening?
- What is reserve capital and why is it critical to obtain?
- Do you know what you are getting into?

new business, and invited them over. (Yes, back in the day we were the precursors to all the telephone sales vermin and spam everybody now despises.) Those final days prior to the grand opening are now a blur of anticipation, pressure, pride…and vacuuming.

Opening night was a blizzard—literally, a once-in-many-a-moon winter storm. You can cross your fingers, close your eyes, and just jump right into an opening. However, it is far better to have a couple of "plan B" alternatives should the "snow hit the fan." We were not that smart. (Heckfire, we didn't even have enough business sense to know what a "soft opening" was.)

After spending the whole day hand-wringing and puckering unseen body parts, we resorted to praying for a change in the weather. The weather did not give us a break, but the universe did. Our talentless hype was so successful in saturating the market that people drove roundabout routes on surface roads to bypass the blizzard-closed highway to attend the opening night. They walked, cross-country skied, and four-wheeled through the snow to partake in our highly buzzed-about virgin business.

It was after that glorious night that we provided ourselves with some new "rules of engagement." Some might call it "Buck Wild."

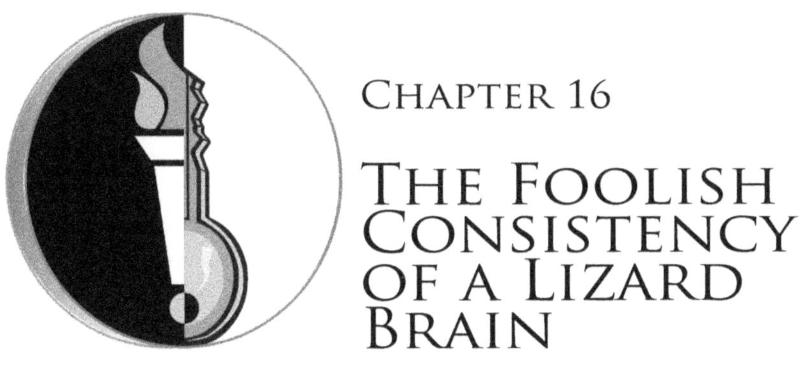

Chapter 16
The Foolish Consistency of a Lizard Brain

Zoom! Bang! Pow! We were on our way, and yes, along that way we indulged in some "behaviors." Imagine, if you will, two red-blooded American males in their early twenties throwing a party every night. I like to think of it this way—*impulsiveness maimed me and responsibility saved me.*

Our families gifted us with a strong sense of right and wrong. We had functioning moral compasses and a burning desire to be successful businesspeople; the team was tight and worked well together. All of the above would not have been enough to keep the dark circus of temptation from taking me far from home if I had not really bought into the concept of professionalism.

How would the world perceive us as businesspeople? That question entered my mind every single night. Our words, actions, and attitudes and the appearance of our establishment were the things that I initially cared about. I could not have faced myself if I had taken the weight of my responsibilities lightly—holding a liquor license, earning a monetary return for our investors, meeting the biweekly payroll, and ensuring our guests had a positive experience.

This high-minded motivation did not, however, deter me from being a moody egoist, an immaturity poster child given to anger outbursts I was convinced were my divine right as the co-ring leader of the aforementioned circus. All of that changed, however, when I blew my right ring finger bone through the back of my shattered hand.

I was basically a good person and a rookie manager who, under pressure, lost my brains. Everyone I had ever worked for had played the boss card with an extra-heavy hand. *Let 'em know with your fire-breathing outbursts just how you are "feeeeling."* The result was complete confusion concerning my desire to be feared, rather than being competent or well-respected.

They say personal change happens when you are ready. I accelerated my readiness on a night I was blind with fury.

One Friday evening during the course of business, a miscreant had stolen a large picture off the wall. (Giant pictures of celebrities were our main décor items.) This was an unprecedented loss; however, my fuming was directed more at my shirking tribemates and their subsequent blame-throwing, "It's his fault. No, it's theirs." I felt compelled to show the staff that this would not stand. *"All eyes better be on the job from here on out!"* I yelled angrily. I cussed bitterly, stomped around, and toppled a trashcan full of empty beer bottles.

Still not feeling as if I had sufficiently exorcized enough demons, I dug into my bag of masculine tricks and decided I needed to punch something. *I'm going to show them just how pissed off I can be!* Having previously punched my share of lockers, walls, and intoxicated combatants (and walking away unscathed) only served to engage the reptilian autopilot mechanism deep within my brain. (For all those concerned about balance in the universe, in the ensuing years I have been flat-out clocked a few times myself.)

So there was the target: the broadside of our filing cabinet. *That will make a hell of a noise, and if I am lucky, a large dent that will forever serve to remind those who pass by, "Never provoke his mighty wrath."*

KA-POW! Or was it THH-WONK? Nah, it was bunk...followed by "MOTHER F'ER!"

I'm not sure if I was a step too close or a step too far away, but my roundhouse punch landed squarely into the reinforced corner edge of the new, spontaneously christened, don't-let-your-mind-write-a check-that-your-hand-can't-cash file cabinet. "Jeezzzuzzz, that hurts! Man that was dumb!" Okay, repeat those two sentences seventy times in one minute, and you'll have an idea of how fast I came to the realization I was in need of some personal changes.

Now let's not pull out the judgment card too quickly on this blatant act of foolishness (as if you were "all that and a bag of chips" in your early twenties). Besides, having all my right fingers morph into extra large hot dogs and then having a permanent metal plate surgically installed to shore up my missing knuckle is, I assure you, payback enough.

My hair-trigger anger habit did not disappear overnight. It was a gradual thing that came to me after a few weeks of not being able to eat properly or write my name. It might have also been the daily positioning of a garbage bag on my arm to take a one-handed shower, or it could have been the troublesome and humiliating obstacle of not being able to work the gearshift in my car. Perhaps it was the procession of other major inconveniences, including severe constipation brought on by my new best friend, Tylenol with codeine. Suddenly a glimmer of intelligence broke through the fog of low (heavy on the codeine, remember...).

I found myself saying, "The stupid stuff has got to go."

If your anger pot is constantly boiling over (i.e., temper tantrums, road rage, work rage, acting out, and so on), you have yet to learn self-control, discipline, maturity, and foresight. Your judgment in all pressure-packed matters should be questioned. Saying it is your nature, or your way, does not excuse the fact that you are indulging in adolescent behavior. You will be setting the example, tone, and boundaries for all of the people whom you influence. (Most dogs that are beaten get mean and are looking for something to bite.)

Rage is not a healthy or becoming habit. In business (we are not talking about a bar fight or a battlefield), it is a waste of precious energies. And be fair warned, you will never get the best people to work for you (that is, unless you pay through the nose or they are masochists—and forget about any chance of loyalty).

I will wrap up this sermon with the following quote from a rather thoughtful world observer:

"A foolish consistency is the hobgoblin of little minds..."
—Ralph Waldo Emerson, Essays First Series, *1841,*
"Self Reliance" (Reading "Self Reliance" is an absolute requirement for all would-be entrepreneurs.)

BROKEN AWAKE

After evaluating my failure to play nice with the other kids, I found myself at the *trough of mindfulness*. We are all guided here from time to time, but we do not always arrive thirsty. This time I was parched with dry, cracked lips. I had taken a rather roundabout route to drink in deeply the fact that the dual challenge of becoming a good leader and a good manager is rather vexing to most people.

A classic conflict arises in business settings—the so-called hard and soft skills of management chafing against each other. If you are good with finances or equipment, you have hard skills. If you are good with people or are creative, you have soft skills. Setting aside the right-brain versus left-brain arguments, the most important thing is to determine what your *natural tendencies tend to be.*

Do you become fired up about the prospect of finding an extra 1 percent savings in cost categories, or do you favor taking a high-potential dishwasher and developing him or her into your next chef?

Before you try to master the whole left-right management enchilada, hire or partner with someone who counterbalances your weaknesses with his or her strengths. This way you can be exposed to opposite views within a constructive environment. If you have apprenticed long and hard with experts on both sides of the coin (you rare bird, you), then—and only then—should you give it a go on your own.

Proprietorship—like many endeavors—is fraught with peril, yet the most fortunate aspect is often overlooked. You can invent, or reinvent as the case may be, your style of management-leadership as you shape the destiny of the enterprise. Yes, this sounds like difficult extra work (Isn't the removal of bad habits always distasteful?) piled on top of your other duties, but if not now, when? Seize the opportunity to discover a stronger set of motivational drivers to achieve the goals set before you.

I am big on words because they are the tools that sculpt ideas. Over the years, many words have become my guide. Maybe you are a reader, maybe you are not. No matter—*somehow* you have to get fresh ideas into your head. Surf the 'Net; subscribe to trade publications; find a mentor, a peer group, or retired advisors—but don't continually tread down the same path and expect rapid professional growth.

I was fortunate to be broken awake. It caused me to concern myself with how to be, as well as what to do. If you have ascended to the responsibility level of leading a team to group success, you must realize the following:

Remember, the things that you want, the things that you do, and the manner in which you do them must be in positive alignment.

Hey, you point out, there are plenty of angry, difficult near-psychopaths who have made it in business. To that, I say, they have been *lucky* until now. They will pay for bad behavior at some point (with their health, if nothing else) and really, this is not the richest way to live. Sometimes change agents have to be rough to shake off ingrained behaviors for turnarounds and desperate survival situations, but the majority of businesses are just looking for wins—not more jerks.

Why? Because, in addition to carrying keys, hiring, firing, paying bills, and driving sales, you become the sun, the light, and the energy source for the business. If you burn brightly and positively, the business has a chance. If you are dim and negative, you are contributing to its demise. People in general do learn best by observation. This means that your actions must speak louder than your words and be moving in the direction that you wish everyone to go.

Here's the starting point. Become excellent at *painting the wins* (communicating a clear picture of what success looks like and how to get there) and *fostering the wins* (teaching or promoting winning skill sets and providing the proper tools) to enable the winners. If a person knows what a win looks like for his or her job and how to get there without your being right in his or her pocket, then you are free to handle the bigger problems.

(Pssst...you can get more done this way.)

If you still think of this as less than important or serious, consider whether you know of one person who is not familiar with the concept of winners and losers, then ask yourself if you know of one person (who is mentally healthy) who would prefer being referred to as a loser. It is basic playground logic—the "me, me, me, pick me for the good team" psychology that is innate in almost everyone.

Here is the real bonus to this concept. As the *leadager*, you frame the picture of these wins. If the group is strong, target the big goals. If not, shoot for smaller goals. You are expected to set the tone, targets, and pace. No matter how small or large the business (or jobs within), the majority of people see themselves as wanting to win and hoping to work for a winner. That is why every second of your behavior and every word in the workplace count. And please, do not forget to do a victory dance with the tribe for memorable milestones achieved along the way.

FARM CHORES

The above is, of course, a basis for the statement that "in business nothing beats experience." An individual becomes seasoned over time (no matter how many times I say it, know in your heart that I'm not plugging my own line of spice), and as events unfold, he or she begins to draw from similar previous encounters; in so doing, he or she shifts from unfamiliar to familiar responses.

At some point you will come to the realization that no matter how badly you want it, no one else is ever going to be *you* with your same desires, goals, and motivations. In a shared workplace there will always be people who simply don't even try to earn their money. There will also be folks who try their hardest and still can't perform well. Not surprisingly, there will also be people with whom you work (above you and below you on the organizational chart) who could do your job better than you if they wanted to.

If you are being paid to be a *leadager*, you are also being paid to keep the following scenario in the forefront of your mind.

You are the closest thing to a farmer outside the natural world. You pick the seeds (hiring), you plant the seeds (training), and you bring the sun (job opportunity/direction) and the

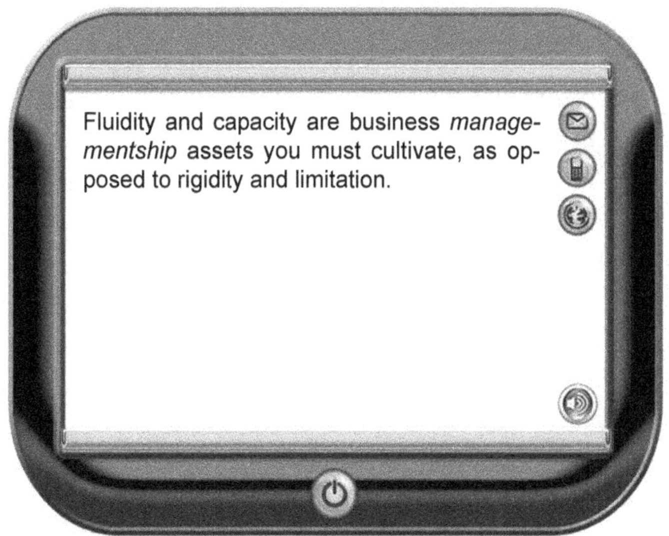

rain (tools/support). You plan for harvest (promotability) and you pull the weeds (firing) from your field. If you are a business farmer (yup, you are) and dead serious about your success, then when you see a seed (or a person on your payroll), you had better see *the potential for what that seed can become*. That's right—the color of your tribe's potential is not the color of their skin or their age, gender, height, or experience. The number of prize-winning tribemates you are able to grow from seeds will certainly play a lion's share of the role in determining the outcome of your business fate.

Meeting topics:

- How do you define professionalism?
- Do you have anger pot problems?
- How often do you reflect on your behavior? Often enough to chart a new course if necessary?
- How do you regenerate your business mind?
- What are the farm chores of a *leadager*?
- Do you put real muscle into increasing your fluidity and capacity?

You want me to dump all my hard-earned biases and prejudices? Jumping Jehosaphat! As a *leadager*, you have to make room for all the stuff flying at you and this biased baggage will weigh you down. *I have seen more damage done in the workplace by biased people dead-set on proving their preconceived prejudices than by anyone who was lumped into a bad person stereotype based on their appearance* (unless we include the facts that smokers desire more work breaks and those hooked on drugs are not in their right mind).

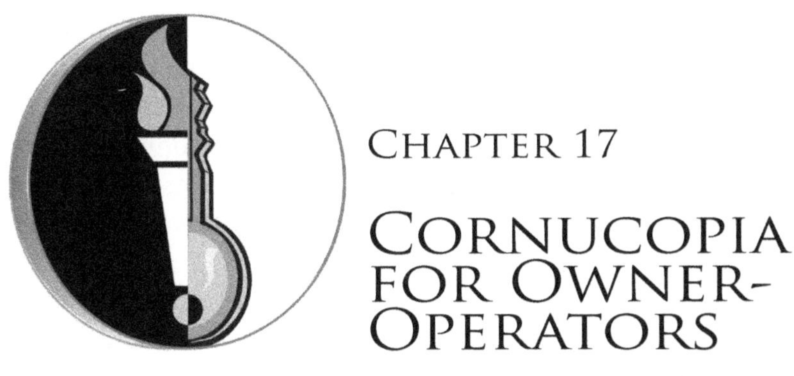

Chapter 17

Cornucopia for Owner-Operators

Our small venture taught me a ton about business. But most importantly, I stumbled upon—and was profoundly impacted by—the realization that *one must really—stretch—in—order—to—accelerate—professional—growth.*

Through the years, we experienced the demise and rejection of "disco" music, our main product offering. We incubated a dancing diversity response to that decline by musically styling different nights of the week to appeal to separate demographic groups (oh sooo novel at the time). We successfully produced live music concerts, pool tournaments, fashion shows, beach parties, holiday bashes, and balloon money drops.

Our "ladies night" promotion was quite successful until it was outlawed because it was deemed "gender discrimination" by the PC police. We responded to that by forming a troupe of male dancers to entertain the ladies without "specials" deemed to be sexist. Punk rock came and went. Country music came and stayed. (Sure 'nuff, most of them cowboys worshiped at the longneck altar.)

Our partnership with a locally infamous, ex–college football player produced a fabulously funky after-hours party, resulting in some notoriety. The "buzz" from this promotion drew a crowd from a completely new demographic. Our new patrons were grateful for a place of business that catered to their tastes without the stereotypical small-minded hassles. We did have to frisk patrons for weapons (so *that* was different), but from the outset we gave respect and received it in return.

We always faced strong price competition and a location disadvantage—the back of a shopping center gives you no roadway visibility. (Duh, what were we thinking?) We also faced absolute animosity directed toward us from the bordering apartment complex. (Who really wants a party bar within sight and sound of your abode?) But mostly, we struggled to try to stay relevant after being continuously broadsided by changing consumer tastes.

Like all small businesses, it felt as if there was a major battle to be fought every day, or at least every week. We were fueled by the dream and pleased by the novelty, but disheartened by the lack of personal wealth we were generating. The lack of vacation time, the sheer ludicrousness of requesting a sick day, and the out-of-the-question retirement program may have contributed to some of the luster wearing off of our endeavor.

Ownership freedoms and perks may never outweigh the headaches unless you are making *a lot* of money.

Yes, it is irrefutably exciting to have a gigantic sound system pumping tunes through your workplace. However, you will gradually despise all popular songs about the 175th time you hear them. Additionally, the awful truth is that if your ears hurt after work, you are hurting them, and other people's smoke in your workbox will hurt your lungs. After a while, wading into bar fights starts to feel less American Gladiator and more American idiot.

The majority of our business was at night, which is a "day part" limited to the time without the sun when most "normal" people are in bed and was skewed toward the two or three nights that people might actually go out. (Breakfast/lunch or lunch/dinner concepts will always give you a chance to draw from a broader market than late night, since two shots at a target are always better than one. Also, it's obvious that most people eat two to three times a day, and if you're lucky they may go out a couple times a week, which is why there are more restaurants than bars.)

Three years later we sold the business (used equipment, sweat equity, and a lease) at a happy profit we were gleeful to take. The new absentee owners closed the business about a year later. (Hmm…owners who were not present, and therefore, not sweating every detail, every day. Could there possibly be a connection?)

Takeaways for owner/operators:

- Never underestimate the powerfully positive vibe that emanates from bringing a viable hospitality business to life. You are bringing jobs to the area. You are quenching a deep hunger and thirst that go far beyond food and drink, including socialization, celebration, and connection. You are supporting the community by paying taxes and any additional community goodwill service or product offering that you choose to provide. If you grow your people well, you have a chance to positively affect the future of your company and your community. If you manage to produce a profit, you might get a chance to *keep it* and *keep at it.*

- Do not rush into owning your own place. The more competent and successful you are at multiple jobs within the industry, the easier it will be to obtain money. As you become more bankable, the less "bank" you will personally have to risk. Excellence will always attract interest.
- Just because you *can* doesn't mean you *should.* You might have the idea, experience, desire, money, and location all lined up, but unless you have an absolute determination to do whatever it takes to make it happen, or an absolute psychosis about working for other people, don't start your own business! Making good money at it has to be a "pretty darn sure" rather than a "surely hope to" proposition. It is a lot more work than you know, without a lot of down time. You will screw up many lives, including your own, if you do not pull it off.
- Determine a realistic financial game plan—the earlier the better. Know every aspect of costs and controls—fixed costs (unaffected by sales volume changes), variable costs (clearly linked to business volume changes), and prime costs (food, beverage, payroll, payroll taxes, and benefits). Overanalyze every aspect and know what your breakeven point is from the "git go" by having a solid proforma.
- Before passing go, can you get legal exclusivity or complete control of your brand? Is there a part of your idea that allows you to dominate your competition? Can you illustrate a limited downside for investors? Do you have a solid plan for taking on economic downturns? Does your plan include wiggle room for unforeseeable missteps? What is the period to profitability or rate of return on investment? Can you show

the commitment and brilliance of the main players? How fast can it get big? How big can it get? These are some of the things that any experienced investor will want to know.

- Plan the divorce before the kiss—partners, investors, and relatives will all turn nasty if reality steps in to "jack up" your planned success. Be sure there is a legal agreement that specifically points the way to move others out, or for you to move on, before you take a penny of other people's money.
- Grow skinny. Startups almost always underestimate expenses and overestimate income. Try to have the business lose expense weight while gaining sales weight in the first year. Hold on to as much of your bottom line profits as you can. This is actually easier than trying to generate more gross sales while under duress.
- You must focus your business efforts on those things that provide for the best chance to get people talking about you. The *big five differentiators* are (1) great product, (2) great value, (3) excellent service, (4) great location, and (5) sensationally brilliant decor. (We might now have to include data mining expertise and relationship-marketing flair, but let's stay old-school for a minute.) Bear in mind that you can be blessed with all "original" five and still not make any money. (Conversely, you can own a "hole in the wall" and be rolling in dough.) Our industry has been built by idea pirates who trolled around the world seeking the next big thing to bring back to their locale. This approach can help you generate ideas for your spot—or it can hurt you if a competitor *clones* your concept.
- Piggyback onto attractions that are located in high-traffic areas. If possible, avoid buying or leasing locations in the middle of nowhere (backstreets, basements, and so forth) just because you finagled some cheap rent (unless you are in a super-major metropolitan area). People are creatures of habit. Industry insiders know that there is no guarantee guests will visit the left side of the establishment if they are seated on the right, but most will hit the bathrooms, making that travel path a good place to market upcoming events. Cities and neighborhoods are the same. Do your homework. If you can, visibly plant your business in a traffic pattern in/next to an entertainment

attraction, intersection, neighborhood, highway, or transit hub that draws a high-volume of your target audience. You cannot afford to hope you'll change people's habits. I have heard of contrarians/visionaries who have "gone on ahead," predating an area's popularity, and have actually played a role in revitalization or rerouting traffic. Some people have also won multimillion dollar lottery jackpots. I just have never met anyone from either of these two lucky groups. As far as I'm concerned, they both could be urban myths. You are already risking a lot by virtue of starting a small business, so be careful and wise.

- Dream big but sweat the details. Manage your cash and work the operations as if you want to have a thousand locations and never intend to sell. This is also known as "keeping your eye on the ball" while developing an exit strategy. If you produce a successful business legacy, you will be approached to expand or sell. You can then decide to stay or go while you are still rising. This is the best of all scenarios.
- High-volume, spirited-beverage establishments with dancing (nightclubs) *are in the fashion trend business;* do not expect them to be a long-term play. (Do you remember last year's hot color, phone of choice, killer song, hemline, etc.?) Nightclubs and trendy bars, if successful, will be beat to death by the party, or the traffic, and will be forced to update *FF&E* within three years. The demand for a freshening could be even sooner if the music, theme, or styles of the moment shift during your run.
- Get the best lawyer, accountant, and insurance agent you can afford, but only if they are referred to you by a trusted source.
- Pay your friggin' taxes.

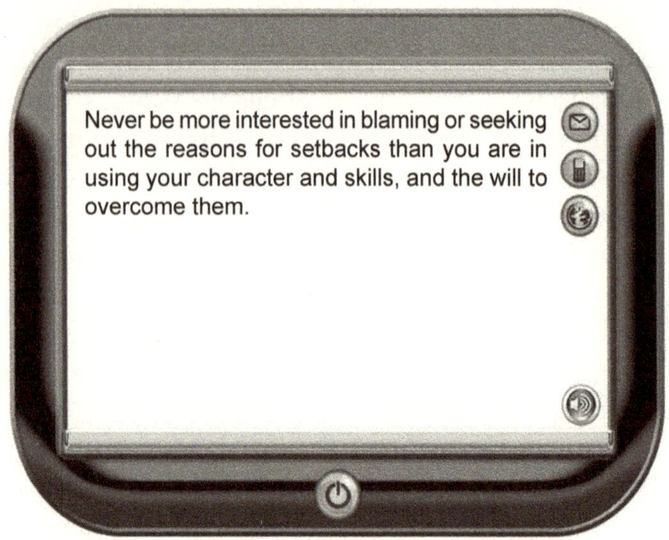

Cattle Drive Zen

(Also applicable for owner/operators)

Protect the herd
If you get bucked off…git right back on
Carry a sharp knife and a sharper set of eyes
Keep your socks and bullets dry
Conserve your jerky and water
Eat when you are hungry
Sleep as much as you can, when you can
Wear a hat in the sun but not in a house
Never gamble with strangers
Don't take any wooden nickels
Be kind to kids and your horse
Ride with pride
Sing a little at night
Never slap leather in anger
Don't make friends with rattlers
Don't give a tinker's damn about what a tenderfoot thinks of you
And find yourself a hootenanny at the end of each drive

Meeting topic:

All the above is fodder for conversations between owner/ operators and themselves or their partners.

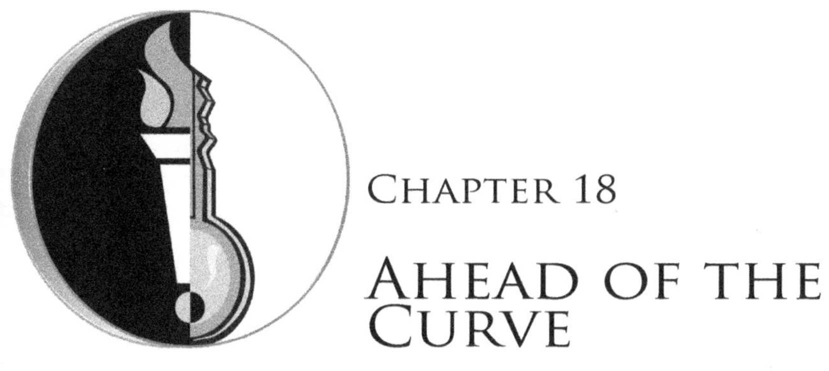

Chapter 18

Ahead of the Curve

You likely have a priority system for responding to e-mails, phone calls, complaints, shopper reports, and suggestion box. As you continue to run your "own" property, however, there will be layer upon layer of information and multiple must-do's that, on a daily basis, can drown out and push the items that must be tracked on a quarterly or annual basis to the background.

"Evergreen" is what I call information you do not need to reference every day but is relevant to running a top-flight hospitality operation. Consider it your "tickler file."

Grab a calendar or spend time inserting the following helpful tickles into your manager's logbook, handheld communication device, or office computer schedules.

- All periods of labor transitions (when school is in/out, holidays, street fests, three-day weekends, in season, out of season, and any changes in labor or par levels)
- All license renewal dates
- All contract renewal dates (leases, beer line cleaning, rental property, store cleaning, music, *CO2,* etc.)
- All equipment maintenance dates (recharge fire extinguishers, summer/winterize *HVAC* systems, first aid kits, air filter switch out, etc.)
- Annual forecasting/budget deadline dates
- Capital improvement expense request (read repair/maintenance issues) deadlines
- Obtain biannual signatures (read and acknowledge) for em-

ployee policy handbook, including harassment policy and grievance resolution procedures

- Notice necessary lead time for all change in hours of operation (post-holiday hours for guests, even if there are no changes from regular hours, to remind people you will be open)
- Open dates for periodic revalidations of uniform requirements
- Reminder to undertake high-dusting biannually (lamps, conduits, ceiling vents/tiles, etc.)
- Instruct garbage service to change out trash dumpsters at least once a year
- Quarterly (at least) dusting, vacuuming, and clean-wipe of audio/visual equipment
- Renew and refresh posted reminders of preventive measures for overconsumption of alcoholic beverages
- Pick dates for reminders/testing of preferred methods for checking identification for alcoholic beverage service
- A couple week's advance notification for daylight savings time change (if applicable) and how you handle alcoholic beverage service with one more/less hour available
- Choose a tentative patio open date (counting forward from the time necessary to hire/train additional tribe members and what/when supplies need to be received)
- Reminder to get on the local pest control schedule for spring and summer ant, fly, nit (and rodent?) control
- Mandatory change dates chosen for passwords, safe combinations, and alarm codes
- All advance preparations for any national sports playoff/finals
- Reminder to alter business traffic plans during income tax week (or any other known sales downers)
- Preplan all monthly staff meetings a minimum of three months in advance
- Set aside time monthly for a safety committee meeting
- Select a time frame to undertake human resource (tribe) paperwork file audits
- Make available regularly scheduled first aid, responsible beverage service, and sanitation classes
- Select energy conservation program start dates (water in the summer/gas and electric in the winter, but hopefully always ongoing)

- Preparations itemized for store birthday/anniversary party
- Make way for the flu season, a *POS* crash (cash register) burglar alarm response, or any unforeseen circumstances/crises where a proper reaction may involve pretraining
- Note open enrollment dates for company-wide programs, such as insurance, 401(k), and so forth
- Preplan menu rewrites
- Select proper time frames for the revisiting of the minimum wage/tip reporting laws

As you can see, this could go on and on! Based on your operation's needs, customize and complete this list with items that fit your time, place, and circumstances.

Be sure to include a biannual planning schedule for each month's operational meeting topics running six months ahead (i.e., safety and security, cleanliness and sanitation, service and sales), then reinforce the topic with pre-shift meetings, surprise quizzes for cash, or some other spiffy contest that you have been dying to roll out.

95 Things to Learn Before You Need 'Em…

1. How to obtain/maintain good mental and physical health and a semi-sunny disposition
2. How to speak confidently in front of a group of people
3. How to take *valid* criticism without becoming overly defensive or overreacting
4. How to "smell the smoke" and respond immediately rather than waiting to "see the fire" (literally and figuratively)
5. How to memorize names and other people's personal minutia
6. How all the food and drinks on your menu should look and taste if plated or glassed and prepared properly
7. How to price menu items to yield a gross percentage target
8. How to rank menu items onto a sales contribution continuum
9. How to standardize and "cost out" food and beverage recipes
10. What to do when you (or somebody else) locks the keys in the office
11. Why it is better to say "heart of the house" than "back of the house"
12. Which booth offers the best sleeping accommodations when

you draw a "back to back" or "clopen" shift

13. How to notice a light bulb is burned out inside your place… without looking up
14. How to "teach" a *P&L*
15. How to memorize your monthly budget targets
16. How to calculate food and beverage cost percentages without a computer or calculator
17. What you are currently "running" for labor cost percentages, by department
18. How to make classic "cocktails" with a mixing tin (the old-fashioned way)
19. The difference between good and bad wine
20. Be able to name and describe ten different pasta types
21. Be able to name and describe ten different cheese types
22. How to find liquid and ladle equivalents
23. Your mayor/city council members, by name
24. The president of the nearest restaurant association, by name
25. The police officers on your "beat," by name
26. Your local food reviewer by sight, or at least by name and dislikes (This is why newspapers, if your city still has one, have archives.)
27. How beer is made
28. The difference between ale, bock, lager, and stout
29. How to "temp check" tap beer
30. What to do if your glycol compressor fails
31. How to systemize "label, date, and rotate"
32. What sanitizer is and why it's in a mini-bucket
33. What the proper "shelf life" is of your products
34. Why cross contamination is bad and hand washing is good
35. Cooking temperature safety zones
36. Where to procure quality bread, fish, and produce
37. How to purchase commodities, and if need be, negotiate an annual contract
38. The grades and cuts of meat or fish
39. How to "check in" or receive a product delivery
40. Who to call if you received the wrong product order
41. How to calibrate a thermometer
42. How to do a meaningful "line check"

43. How to work a position on the line and not drag the kitchen down
44. How to make a thick milkshake or a "half-caff" latte
45. How to put the hand guard on the mixer and slicer
46. How to set up/break down a pizza oven, flat-top, or grill
47. How to set-up/break down your dishwashing machine
48. How to speak Spanish or the predominate local kitchen language
49. How properly to use chopsticks and silverware ("continental style")
50. Whether your tribe has all the proper tools to do the jobs you need them to do
51. Why energy conservation, "the green dream," heart happy, recycling, organically grown, and vegetarians are mainstream, not "way out there"
52. What to do if the *POS* crashes
53. What to do if there is a phone call "bomb threat"
54. What to do if someone calls you requesting money for a ruined suit, making them sick, or an injury due to your alleged negligence
55. Who to call if the walk-in cooler dies
56. Who to call if the *HVAC* dies
57. Where the fire sprinkler shut-off valve is located
58. How to clean up after a hood fire suppression system accidentally discharges
59. Where to get ice at night if the ice machine dies
60. The number of a plumber who works at night
61. The Heimlich maneuver
62. How to interview someone without making an illegal misstep
63. How to review someone without making an illegal misstep
64. How to set up performance plans and goals for individuals and groups
65. How to provide progressive discipline without making an illegal misstep
66. How to terminate someone without an illegal misstep
67. How to calm a chef or *KM*
68. The names of five hospitality recruiters (for the benefit of yourself and the property, especially handy if the chef doesn't calm down)
69. How to solicit a raise in pay

70. What *ASCAP/BMI* are and why they matter
71. What a tip credit is (or any other available government-related job credits)
72. How to take and confirm a large party reservation
73. How to mop a bathroom or sweep a parking lot
74. How to maintain clean restrooms that smell nice
75. How to run a frequent visitor, birthday, gift card, and business card database/program
76. How to write a sincere letter of apology
77. How to write a press release
78. How to draft a logo that isn't stupid
79. How to catch someone stealing from you
80. How to get everyone working for you on "the same page" with daily, weekly, and monthly specials, sales goals, and system improvement focus
81. How to model proper greetings and "send-offs" to guests
82. How to take an efficient and accurate inventory
83. Why the sound of breaking glass or the sight of black smoke or a wet floor should trigger instant action on your part
84. How to monitor and properly respond to "ticket times," "table turns," "guest counts," and "comment card" reports, shift-by-shift, week-by-week
85. How to "expo" and "run" food
86. Never send female tribemates out to their cars alone late at night
87. The "feel it in your bones" definitions of store blind, guest eyes, blown-away-by-the-experience, and sexual harassment
88. To make it a point to regularly attend trade shows and read trade publications
89. How to conduct a "competition research" visit
90. How to slip into your main competitors' promotional e-mail, snail-mail, social network, or text message list
91. Details that define "favorable location"
92. Details that define "favorable lease"
93. How to write a mission statement or victory vision, roll it out, and make it stick
94. How to write a business plan and to rewrite a business plan into a *realistic* business plan
95. The difference between activities and accomplishments

SUGGESTED READINGS AND RESOURCES

RECOMMENDED READING

The Experience Economy: Work Is Theatre and Every Business Is a Stage by B. Joseph Pine II and James H. Gilmore. HB Press: Boston, 1999.
This book recast my view of the hospitality/service industry. It can change your priorities.

Simplicity: The New Competitive Advantage in a World of More, Better, Faster by Bill Jensen. Perseus Books: Cambridge, Mass., 2000.
After reading this book, clarity becomes the top priority when one hopes to advance an agenda.

The Republic of Tea: How An Idea Becomes a Business—Letters to a Young Zentrepreneur by Mel Ziegler, Bill Roenzweig, and Patricia Ziegler. Currency/Doubleday: New York, 1992.
A diary of a successful start up by way of letters from a business mentor to his junior partner. The lessons are zen-ish but memorable.

The Great Game of Business by Jack Stack with Bo Burlingham. Currency/Doubleday: New York, 1992.
A very enlightening explanation of how one business turned from the brink of failure into a roaring success through the use of open book management

The Art of Profitability by Adrian Slywotzky. Warner Business Books: New York, 2002.

An extraordinary look at a multitude of possibilities for you to increase the profits for your business.

Raving Fans: A Revolutionary Approach to Customer Service by Kenneth Blanchard and Sheldon Bowles. William Morrow: New York, 1993.
A wonderfully simple customer service classic.

Leadership and the One Minute Manager: Increasing Effectiveness Through Situational Leadership by Ken Blanchard, Patricia Zigarmi, and Drea Zigarmi. William Morrow: New York, 1985.
This book presents a novel approach to effective leadership, but it is imperative to practice its precepts on a continual basis or you will lose touch quickly.

Orbiting the Giant Hairball: A Corporate Fool's Guide to Surviving with Grace by Gordon MacKenzie. Viking/Penguin Group- New York, 1998.
A wacky view of how things move inside of an organization through the eyes of a creative master craftsperson.

Purple Cow: Transform Your Business By Being Remarkable by Seth Godin. Portfolio/Penguin Group: New York, 2003.
A small book with a big idea about business marketing.

Kitchen Confidential: Adventures in the Culinary Underbelly by Anthony Bourdain. ECCO/Harper Collins: New York, 2000.
Insiders look a chef's life in New York City with trade secrets and titillating stories; so successful it brought Mr. Bourdain his own TV show.

The Hospitality Law Desk Reference by Elio C. Bellucci, J.D. Southern Beverage Journal, Inc.: Atlantis, Fla., 1994.
A hard-to-come-by, hospitality industry insider's guide used for risk management and liability assessment. Eye-opening bear traps!

Dinosaur Bar-B-Que: An American Roadhouse by John Stage and Nancy Radke. Ten Speed Press: Berkeley, 2001.
Motorcycle ruffians turned restaurateurs, the origins of a true American classic joint. Buy it for the recipes and you will rule over all backyard grillers.

INDUSTRY RESOURCES

National Restaurant Association
1200 17th Street, NW, Washington, D.C. 20036; 202-331-5900
www.restaurant.org
Click through to "Profitability & Entrepreneurship," then click through to "Industry Trade Publications," and find a treasure trove of linked industry information topic by topic.

Nations Restaurant News
425 Park Avenue, New York, NY 10022; 212-756-5000
www.nrn.com
Almost everyone I know subscribes to this trade magazine. A broad overview of news, trends, and opinions about the industry.

Hotel F&B Magazine
www.hotelfandb.com
Proudly serves lodging food and beverage professionals in hotels, resorts, and casinos worldwide.

Job Hunting

www.hcareers.com
nrnjobplate.com
www.careerbuilder.com
www.mthrailkill.com
www.theelliotgroup.com
www.usajobs.gov

Supplies

www.foodservice.com
www.restaurantowner.com
www.anything4restaurants.com
www.profitablehospitality.com

Education

www.cookingschools.com
www.allculinaryschools.com
www.ciachef.edu
www.chefs.edu

Of Interest

www.fohboh.com
Front of the House & Back of the House community site

www.culinarycult.com
A portal to the hospitality world

www.chowhound.com
Delicious chat site

www.bighospitality.co.uk
British take on hospitality

www.starchefs.com
Magazine for culinary insiders

www.foodnetwork.com
TV shows galore

www.recipesource.com
Searchable online recipe archive

bafoodist@bonappetit.com
Restaurant editor Andrew Knowlton

www.acfchefs.org
American Culinary Federation

www.ahla.com
American Hotel and Lodging Association

www.chef2chef.com
A chef's guide to everything (almost)

www.hospitalitynet.org
Global newsletter

www.mfha.net
Multicultural Foodservice & Hospitality Alliance

www.nightclub.com
Nightclub and bar magazine

www.elance.com
Hire, manage, and pay experts to do your work

sethgodin.typepad.com
Author, provocateur, noteworthy blogger

www.b2byellowpages.com
Business-to-business directory

www.foodbooks.com
Serious books for serious cooks

www.aiwf.com
American Institute of Wine and Food

www.dinnersfromhell.com
Dining disasters in all their gory detail

www.andrewzimmern.com
Travel Channel host and former chef

Restaurants for Sale
www.restmart.com
www.natbiz
www.franchising.com
www.francorp.com
www.franchiseworks.com

AFTERWORD

THIS BOOK IS THE OFFSPRING OF ODD-couple parents—not mine but rather two other forces of the universe (not that my parents weren't): my wife, Kristi, and my passion (not that my wife isn't). As I have shared with Kristi over the past twenty years the dozens of "truth is stranger than fiction" stories, she has always maintained that the hospitality industry should have its own daytime soap opera. Over time, however, and not unexpectedly, she has become less enthralled—and far more repelled—by the strangeness of my tribal tales. Still, in a deep, primordial sort of way, Kristi still occasionally finds my "shop-talk" stories of interest, much like a rubberneck gawker passing by a highway accident. But like any good storyteller whose audience has waned over time—and interest is now feigned—I found myself motivated to search for greener pastures. Lucky you.

As you now know, I am not a celebrity chef—and this is not a cookbook. In fact, I have never chased anyone around a kitchen while wielding a knife—and I happen to think of that as a win.

Prior to creating my hospitality consulting business, I was most recently a regional, multi-unit operator for a national restaurant chain. I began my career, however, where many of my peers dream of ending up—owning a place of my own. I successfully gave that a go as a twenty-one-year-old "know-nothing." Since then, and for almost thirty years, I have had the pain and the pleasure of working for independent operators, national and regional hospitality chains, the U.S. Government Department of Defense as a multi-unit manager for the Army and Air Force Exchange Service, and running a few more places of my own. I have attended management training camps, had articles published in hospitality trade magazines, have given numerous speeches at trade shows, and have won organizational awards. I have opened numerous new stores (closed a few, too) and partnered with thousands of hourly staff members and *a gazillion managers*. Additionally, I have lived through being hired, promoted, bonused, busted-back, and fired. All in all, my ride has been dynamic, fulfilling, and intermittently dysfunctional.

You must find your own way in your own time, just as I did while simultaneously charting my course—whether it was on purpose or by accident. What I did not do, however, is repeat the same mistakes—or the same year of experience—thirty-plus times. As a result, my experience and perspective within the hospitality industry may be worth using as a foundation on which to build. Hopefully, this information has provided you with a new-style "cookbook" of leadership and management recipes. It remains completely up to you to add your own "life seasonings" to suit your own tastes or those of the individuals who sign your paycheck, if that is your goal.

Thanks for the time it took for ya'll to read my book. Now, if you would, kindly go forth and multiply!

www.ingramcontent.com/pod-product-compliance
Lightning Source LLC
Chambersburg PA
CBHW021335090426
42742CB00008B/620

* 9 7 8 0 9 8 4 3 8 1 8 2 1 *